THE

CLARION

CALL

**An Expose of
Satan's Operations
in the Church
in this Final Hour**

Christal Linneman

The Clarion Call, by Christal Linneman

ISBN #0-89228-153-7

Copyright 2005, Christal Linneman

Impact Christian Books
332 Leffingwell Ave.,
Kirkwood, MO 63122
314-822-3309
www.impactchristianbooks.com

Cover Design: *Ideations*

DEDICATION

This book is dedicated first of all to my Lord and Savior Jesus Christ, who has commissioned it, and to the Body of Christ.

Also to my precious husband, Eldrin, called of God to be a sentry by my side.

To our precious children and grandchildren, Mitchell and his wife, Mary, and their children, Miranda and Micah; Janet and her husband, Jack, and their children, Andrew, Quinn, and Grant.

To Geri and Ariel, anointed servants of God sent to confirm my calling.

To Glenda, a precious sister now with the Lord.

To Nancy L. a special friend and prayer partner through the years.

To Pastor Dave and Debra whose love and anointed ministry came during a critical time.

To Lenora and Sharon, the Lord's vessels, sent to my hospital room "to set the grim reaper to flight."

To Darlene E. and her husband, Ken, whose steadfastness has been a source of true inspiration.

To my sister, Iona, and her husband, Norman, along with my husband, Eldrin, and son, Mitch, who have constantly encouraged me to get this book completed. Also special thanks to Mitch and Mary for their hard work and dedication in typing the manuscript and to Nancy D. for the arduous task of final typing.

To Sam and Timmy, special servants, through whom came a recent word, "Get the book finished; time is of the essence."

To all the other precious saints and ministries who have prayed; "and their works do follow them" (Revelation 14:13).

The events of this book are true. Some of the names and places have been changed. All Scripture is taken from the *King James Version* of the Bible, unless otherwise indicated.

TABLE OF CONTENTS

Chapter One

A CALL TO VIGILANCE

"Blow ye the trumpet in Zion, and sound an alarm in my holy mountain: let all the inhabitants of the land tremble: for the day of the Lord cometh, for it is nigh at hand. "
(Joel 2:1)

Set before me is a heavenly mandate. This book must be written in obedience to the Lord, Jesus Christ. I am neither a writer nor a speaker, yet God has called me to write and he has called me to speak out in places where, seemingly, no one else will speak. He is calling me once again to "blow the trumpet," as it were, and to sound the alarm in this late hour. As the clock ticks down to the midnight hour, millions of souls hang in the balance.

Jesus is coming soon! Are you ready to meet Him? Will you be counted worthy to escape the wrath that is to come (Luke 21:36)? Through every possible means, the invitation is being extended to come quickly into the Ark (through the blood of Jesus Christ) before the door is forever closed. We are living in the last of the last days before the Lord's return.

The prophet, Isaiah, describes precisely the time in which we are living. As gross darkness covers the earth, the Lord is calling His chosen ones to arise and shine for His glory (Isaiah 60:1,2). All over the world the Spirit of God is wooing the souls of men before it is eternally too late. Seven times in the second and third chapters of the book of Revelation we find these words: "He that hath an ear, let him hear what the Spirit saith unto the churches." The sleeping church is being aroused and those who have been awakened are being exhorted to stay awake and alert with oil in their lamps and with wicks trimmed (Matthew 25:1-13).

God is no respecter of persons. As He promised to do in Joel 2:28,29, in the last days He is pouring out His Spirit upon all flesh. Anyone who is hungering and thirsting after righteousness can receive the wine and milk without money or price as promised in Isaiah 55:1. As Jesus feeds us of Himself (restoring His gifts and ministries to His body), He is calling us to be His servants and soldiers on the battlefield of spiritual warfare. His eyes sweep to and fro throughout the earth to find those whose hearts are perfect toward Him (II Chronicles 16:9). As He fills the ranks of His army, He looks not for ability but for availability. God's ways are not the ways of man (Isaiah 55:9).

Had someone told me just a few short years ago that God would raise me up and set me into place as an end-time watchman just before Jesus' return, I simply could not have believed. Yet the Lord has shown me I was chosen and ordained for this position in the five-fold ministry of the body of Christ (Ephesians 4:11, I Corinthians 12:28) even before I was formed in the womb (Jeremiah 1:5). When feelings of inadequacy have threatened to overwhelm me, the Lord has gently reminded me that it is not by (my) might nor power but by His Spirit that His work will be accomplished (Zechariah 4:6). He reminds me that I did not choose Him nor the position to which He has called me. He chose me (John 15:16). Had I been given a choice of position, I would have chosen something entirely different!

Regardless of what we may feel or think, God's gifts and calling are without repentance (Romans 11:29). He does not withdraw what He gives simply because we feel inadequate or tremble at the persecution that will surely follow our obedience to Him. Indeed, He can use effectively only those who know they are nothing and can do nothing apart from Him (John 15:5). Over and over His grace has proven sufficient as His strength has been made perfect in my weakness (II Corinthians 12:9).

There can be no visions of grandeur concerning the "lofty" position of the one who "walks the wall." Called to be a servant to both God and man, the watchman learns quickly of the price that must be paid as he takes his place in the Lord's "lookout" tower. Acting as God's spokesman, the watchman must cry out and sound the alarm against the intrusion of the enemy. He must also sound the warning to "repent or perish" before God's impending judgment falls. Opposing the tide of public opinion, he will often walk entirely alone, except for his God, bearing the misunderstanding, persecution and rejection of men.

Because of this calling, my husband, Eldrin, and I know what it means to bear the reproach of Christ – to be ostracized by both family and friends (some to whom life in ministry was freely poured out) who proved untrue. Because of this calling and our subsequent obedience to the Lord, we have borne the humiliation of public excommunication from a church where we held membership and had fellowshipped (in good standing) for over seven years. As a result of the aftermath, we would experience the paralyzing fear (temporary, thanks be to God as we called upon the name of the Lord) of a threat against Eldrin's life. I have been accused of being everything from the exceedingly wicked Jezebel of the Old Testament to a modern-day witch sent by Satan. These words of Jesus have given consolation and strength as well as the comforting assurance of being right on track for the Lord:

> "Blessed are they which are persecuted for righteousness' sake: for theirs is the kingdom of heaven. Blessed are ye,

when men shall revile you, and persecute you, and shall say all manner of evil against you falsely, for my sake. Rejoice and be exceeding glad: for great is your reward in heaven: for so persecuted they the prophets which were before you." (Matthew 5:10-12)

Those who go forward in obedience to the Lord will surely head into Satan's territory. They can expect not only to be falsely accused, but also to meet in head-on confrontations with the powers of darkness. While writing my first book, *There's More to be Had*, literally all of hell rose up in an attempt to destroy the work God had called me to do. Satan did not want to be uncovered through my personal testimony with its prophetic message to the church and he fought viciously, through every possible means, right down to the wire. After publication, I just wanted to put away my writing pen and retire from the battlefield forever, but God had other plans. Quickly, I learned that a soldier in God's army never retires.

Being called to write and publish a book for the Lord was beyond my wildest dreams. I had never written anything to speak of and certainly nothing for publication, so I felt that writing a book would be the epitome of all the Lord would ever call me to do. This feeling, however, did not bear witness with my spirit and before the first chapters were even completed the Lord spoke clearly, "This book is but a 'launching pad' of what I want to do with your life."

Later, when I shared this word with Ginny, a sister in ministry for the Lord, she laughingly exclaimed, "Who wants the launching pad if they can have the blast-off?!" I had no idea of how or when the "blast-off" would occur, but I already knew, deep within my spirit, that something really awesome lay ahead. The Spirit of the Lord had been showing me that it would be something of great magnitude - penetrating and far-reaching in scope.

Little could I know of the events that were to follow. Nor could I dream that the Lord would require yet another book – a book with a subject most hated by Satan (to which the blood of millions of martyrs testify) a book which, I believe the Lord has shown me, will be used as one of His final trumpet warnings before gross darkness, unlike mankind has ever known, covers the earth.

Within the next few years it became easy to see that the writing of a book had indeed been only a launching pad, or foundation, for the "heavier" assignments down the road. Although I had fully intended to "put away my writing pen forever," the Lord made it clear that this book, too, must be written and, since He had given the title for *There's More to be Had*, I began to seek Him diligently for a title for this second book.

One day, after struggling for some time with titles that didn't seem to fit, the word "clarion" kept coming to mind over and over. Suddenly, in the middle of duties, I stopped short knowing the Lord was speaking to me. God has often spoken to me profoundly through one word and the title for this book was no exception. When He had my full attention, letting me know it was He who was speaking, I was directed, as so often in the past, to my dictionary for precise meaning and further illumination of what He wanted me to know.

I'm always excited when God speaks to me and, since I did not know the exact meaning of the word, clarion, the dictionary definition gave even more reason for excitement. Clarion, according to Webster's, means "a trumpet having very clear and shrill tones – loud and clear; as, a clarion call to action"! Since I already knew the Lord had set me as a "watchman unto the house of the Lord" and since I knew the watchman is one who blows the trumpet and sounds the alarm, the definition of the word, clarion, left no doubt as to the urgency of the hour and the purpose for this book. With the hand of God upon me, the phrase, "The Clarion Call" formed very quickly. The Lord confirmed the title by making sure I heard the exact phrase, "the clarion call," twice within the week through separate sources – first, through Pat Robertson on *The 700 Club* and, secondly, through one of the speakers at a James Robison Convention I was attending.

I've often described my walk in the Spirit as a roller-coaster ride with Jesus. About the time I've been able to catch my breath, I've heard the Lord say, "Hold on! Here we go again!" The spiritual warfare has been intense and the sting of persecution is never easy to bear but, oh, how I rejoice when I know, *that I know, that I know* that I've heard the voice of Jesus and have been obedient to Him. It is truly possible to be "exceeding glad" in the midst of tribulation and persecution that come for righteousness' sake.

In this book I will share God's call on my life, some of the fiery trials He has taken me through and the step-by-step assignment given to expose what I believe will be Satan's highest form of deception in this final hour. As I begin to write, I am again very aware of the warfare to be encountered as Satan is exposed. I am also aware of the controversy sure to follow the writing of this book. Only after much prayer and confirmation do I set myself to the task at hand. Only with the Lord's grace, strength, wisdom and protection will this work be completed. I have counted the cost (Luke 14:26-35) and am determined to obey God regardless of the cost. He has told me to set my face like a flint (Isaiah 50:7) in obedience to His call on my life. Again, as with the first book, the Holy Spirit has gently, but firmly, nudged each day to get this work underway and completed. All but basic commitments have been removed in order to free me for this assignment.

We are told in I John 4:1 to test the spirits whether they are of God. Today there are many spirits *within the church* that are not of God. According to II Thessalonians 2:3, a great falling away will precede the coming of the Lord. Very rapidly, Satan is spreading his giant network of delusion over the entire world. The stage is being set for the ushering in of the anti-Christ. Many will be deceived and snared. We are told to be sober and vigilant (I Peter 5:8) for our adversary, the devil, walks about seeking whom he may devour. The entire New Testament is full of warnings. Matthew 24:13 declares that he who endures to the end shall be saved. Eternal vigilance is the price we pay for freedom in Jesus Christ. It is upon this theme that I base the urgent and timely message of this book.

Chapter Two

A MOST UNLIKELY CANDIDATE

"But God hath chosen the foolish things of the world to confound the wise."   *(I Corinthians 1:27)*

I can attest to the fact that there is no power on earth greater than the wooing, convicting power of the Holy Spirit and that when Jesus Christ, so fitly described as "the high sheriff of heaven," apprehends a life by the mighty power of His Spirit that life is forever changed.

Although born and raised in the church, I groped in darkness until the Lord began a work in my life during a three-year period that could, in no way, be attributed to man. This three-year period of intensive teaching and obedience training took place at Ft. Leonard Wood, Missouri during Eldrin's final tour of military duty. Accompanied by insatiable hunger for Jesus and his Word and, finally, total abandonment to God, it culminated in April of 1976 with the mighty baptism in the Holy Ghost and a glorious visit to heaven. Step by step, the Lord led in beautiful ways enabling me to overcome each of Satan's attacks as he fought to keep me from the power of God. How I praise God for His guidance and for His protective hand upon me.

As my hunger kindled, the Lord sent Spirit-filled people into my church - first Ruth, then Don and Marie. I knew nothing of what it meant to be Spirit-filled but these people were different. They carried Bibles! They loved the Word. How I hungered for what they had! About the time I discovered what made Ruth different, I was called upon to teach a children's weekday course entitled "Led by the

Spirit"! Through this course, I saw the crucial need for the Holy Spirit in the church, but fear filled my heart. My church did not teach this "more" for which I hungered. I knew I must obey God rather than man (Acts 5:29) and I learned that God, who is bigger than all the fear the devil can muster, makes a way where there is no way.

God used both Ruth and Marie before they left our area and, later, He again used Ruth to lead me to Gabi (Gabriele!) not of my denomination. By then I was so empty and dry that denominational walls could no longer hold me. The hand of God was heavy upon me and my only prayer had become "use me, Lord." So strong was the Spirit's drawing that I felt I could have flown – or crawled, if necessary, to get to Gabi's house. Speaking right through this precious vessel, with her anointed ministry of agape love and deliverance, the Lord not only laid me bare, but also disclosed the devil's lies. The guilt and condemnation blocking my faith had to go. Later, in my prayer closet, I asked Jesus to baptize me in the Spirit. The devil continued his lies but, praise God, through Gabi, I learned of a little group of Spirit-filled ladies who met (miracle of miracles!) nearby. There, God's power fell as I received the manifestation of the baptism in the Holy Spirit. Never again would I be the same.

From the natural standpoint, it was probably the most inopportune time of my life to hear Jesus say, "Follow Me!" Many changes were taking place in my family all at once with each demanding immediate and undivided attention. Yet everything that I considered important quickly took second place to the Master's call. Overnight, my world had been turned "upside down" by the power of God.

Let me say right here that God wants all of His blood-bought, born-again children baptized in the Holy Spirit (Luke 24:49) with the evidence of speaking in tongues according to Acts 2:4. (If you cannot yield your tongue to the Lord, it is highly doubtful you will be able to yield anything else!) But, oh, how the devil hates the power of God! He will feed you every conceivable lie cleverly twisting the truth of God's Word to keep you from receiving. He knows that without this power you will be of little, if any, threat to him or his kingdom of darkness. He knows, too, that without this power you will never really know what it means to be led by the Spirit of God and you will probably never lead another soul to salvation in Jesus Christ. No wonder Satan hates the power of God!

Those who truly hunger and thirst after righteousness will not twist God's Word. They will accept it in the simplicity in which it is written. Jesus admonishes that unless we become as little children we will never enter the kingdom of heaven (Matthew 18:3)! It takes humility and child-like faith to receive the truths of God. More will be said about pride and about Satan's highest and oldest form of subtlety – the twisting of God's Word – as additional chapters unfold.

Soon after the manifestation of the baptism in the Holy Spirit came an anointing so powerful that I hardly knew how to handle the power within (more on the anointing later). Clothed with power from on high (Acts 1:8) and totally bathed in the love of God, my only desire was to witness for Jesus and to lift Him up as the only way to heaven. The Word of God acquired through the years (mostly through the teaching of children's programs) now became the living Word – "quick and powerful and sharper than any two-edged sword" (Hebrews 4:12).

Here, it must be emphasized that the church without the Holy Spirit is a dead church. And, the Word without the quickening power of the Spirit is nothing more than the dead letter of the law! It has been given unto me to cry out for I have heard the Spirit's solemn warnings: "Woe be to the church that resists and fights the Holy Spirit! Hear what the Spirit saith unto the churches. Repent quickly, while time yet remains for it is God you are opposing! There is only one unforgivable sin and that is the sin against the Holy Ghost" (Matthew 12:31,32). "It is a fearful thing to fall into the hands of the living God" (Hebrews 10:31)!

Those who are comfortable with a dead form of religion on this planet are going to have trouble fitting into heaven – if they make it. There's nothing dead there – only LIFE and JOY that emanate from the Spirit of God! The joy of heaven is absolutely indescribable. Given the blessed privilege of visiting heaven's throne room (two nights after receiving the manifestation of the baptism in the Spirit), I experienced this indescribable joy as I joined the praises of the redeemed. Together, with loud, voluminous, powerful, joyous praise, we worshipped the Lamb who was slain (Revelation 5:11-12). There were multitudes (like rivers of living water!) – yet we were one, in perfect unison. I heard angelic music, too, which no earthly tongue can describe.

Before my spirit left this body of clay to be taken to the third heaven, I lay in a trance-like state upon my bed (see II Corinthians 12:2 and Acts 10:9-17) where I witnessed for what seemed like half the night. Oh, how I witnessed for Jesus as the only way to heaven (see again Acts 1:8) to the streams and streams of people who crossed my path! (In many ways, this vision has been, and is being, fulfilled.)

For days following the visit to heaven, I was literally laid out under the power of God while revelations from the throne room poured over me like waves. Under the shadow of the Almighty, my own mortal strength was taken from me. Coming home for meals, Eldrin would find me (with Bible open by the sink) laid out under God's power on the kitchen floor! I praise the Lord for this special man who stood by me even though he didn't always understand what was happening in my life.

Taken from the dark enclosure of denominationalism and translated into the marvelous light of Jesus Christ, I felt I could fully relate to the Damascus Road experience of the Apostle Paul. Where I had been blind, I could now see. The holy awe and special kinship I had felt while teaching the weekday children about the calling of Isaiah, Jeremiah and Ezekiel now burned in my spirit. Like Isaiah, a coal from God's holy altar had touched my lips. And, as the joy of heaven lifted and a mantle of suffering fell in its place, I was shown that, for my obedience, I would suffer much as did Jeremiah, God's "weeping" prophet of old. So grievous in my spirit was this God-given burden that I wanted to cry out, "Oh, God who am I? I cannot bear this burden! Take it off!"

For three days I was under heaven's sentence of death. Even my countenance took on a death-like pallor. Alarmed by my appearance, Eldrin wasn't sure I should go back to the "Holy Ghost meetings" I'd gotten involved in! But the Lord was at the helm and in control. Not only did He show me what lay ahead for me, but I was shown that severe persecution lay ahead also for all true followers of Jesus Christ. Through a powerful prophecy that left us all sobered and shaken, the word regarding severe persecution and the lateness of the hour was confirmed at the very next prayer meeting.

It would be impossible, I believe, to relate all the revelation I was given within a short period of time. Each part fit together like a puzzle pointing to one spectacular event – the very soon return of the Lord Jesus Christ. The Lord let me know I was in the final great outpouring of His Spirit and that many others would be "swept in right before the bell." He showed me He was going to do a quick work and cut it short in righteousness (Romans 9:28) and that all that could be shaken would be shaken so that that which could not be shaken would remain (Hebrews 12:27). (We are seeing the quick work and the shaking!)

I was shown that the "age of the gentiles" was quickly coming to a close (Romans 11:25) and that God's great prophetic time clock was ticking down over the nation of Israel. (I was not even sure what the age of the gentiles meant!) As my spiritual eyes were opened, I saw, with amazement, that, just as the Jewish people had been scattered all over the world (fulfilling Bible prophecy), they were again being re-gathered to the nation of Israel exactly as prophesied.

With deep foreboding, I sensed the ominous approach of a one-world church and a one-world government system. In my spirit, I heard these words, "They (controlling powers) will be able to find you (people) no matter where you go; there will be no place to hide." At that time, in 1976, I knew little, if anything, about computer technology and certainly nothing about the new age movement. But now it is easy to see how the 666 system is ready to fall into place.

I had never heard end-time preaching in my church, but now I saw that prophetic events such as the rapture, the tribulation, and the millennial reign of Jesus Christ were close at hand. (The devil hates this end-time doctrine and has been very successful in keeping it out of the church.) The terrible holiness of the wrath of God penetrated every fiber of my being as portions of Revelations 14:14-20 were quickened to my spirit. I knew that God's time to "thrust in the sickle and reap" was very near and that the battle lines were being clearly drawn with the countdown to Armageddon. I felt, as it were, the last throes of a sin-sick world groaning and travailing for redemption (Romans 8:21,22). As I sensed the awesome nearness of these climactic events, I knew that mysteries of the word of God, veiled for centuries, were being unveiled for all who have "ears to hear."

How true God is to His Word! In John 16:13 He promises to show us things to come. He not only showed me things to come on a worldwide scale but he revealed things to come in my own personal life and ministry. Had I not tasted of the joy and glory of heaven, I would not have been able to bear what the Lord disclosed. He showed me that my church, the Missouri Synod Lutheran Church, was resisting and even fighting His Holy Spirit – that it was a church that trusted in a form of religion denying the power thereof (II Timothy 3:5). (I always thought we had all there was!) I knew the awful consequences of fighting God and my spirit grieved deeply as I sensed the spiritual death of the multitudes who sit in church pews Sunday after Sunday hell-bound because they have never been born again. I could feel heaven's grieving for the old-fashioned altar call where Holy Ghost conviction could fall, followed by true repentance and the new birth.

With the fire and power of the Spirit, I wanted to win the world for Jesus but, true to His Word, He said, "first in Jerusalem" – *home*! Burdened for my church, for the community where I was born and raised and for a host of unsaved relatives, I thought it would be easier to win the world! The Lord showed me He would send me to my own but that my own would receive me not – that, initially, only one person, my father, would receive my witness. I was shown those who would fight most adamantly – *workers within the church*! Others, with little regard for the church, suddenly became religiously loyal! My witness would go forth, the Lord said, but it would not be received and, as awesome as it seemed, since it was the Lord who was sending me (John 13:20), He showed me that if they did not receive me, they were not receiving Him!

I had never understood why Jesus, the Prince of Peace, said He came not to bring peace but a sword – to set members of a household against one another (Matthew 10:34-39). Now His words were perfectly clear! Fear gripped my heart but He showed me I must be willing to give up both family and church to follow Him.

As I saw the apostate condition of my own church, I was made aware that other denominations were in a similar state. Without His Spirit, the Lord showed me there was no hope. He showed me that judgment would begin in the household of God (I Peter 4:17) and that He was going to sweep through the churches like a fire taking out those who were His own. He made it clear that darkness and light would not dwell together and that the separation of the sheep and the goats had begun. Even now I can sense the teeth that are gnashing against me, but I must say what the Lord has told me to say. Once more, I cry out, "Lord, who am I that you would call me to speak forth such things?"

There is little, if anything, in my life, according to worldly standards, that would qualify me as a candidate for God's use. There are no degrees behind my name and I have never attended a Bible school or college. I grew up on a farm in the midst of a German Lutheran settlement in central Missouri where life in those early years was crude and often cruel. Being of a sensitive nature, I especially felt the pain of things I did not understand. I knew little of earthly comforts or security and nothing, experientially, of the unconditional love of God. Only by revelation would I later see the demonic oppression that rested, not only upon the hill I called home, but over the entire community where I was born and raised. I would also see how profoundly God had had His hand upon my life.

In early childhood, I saw an open vision of Jesus together with my brother, Calvin. An open vision, I understand, is the highest type of vision. The words of the prophet Joel, (Joel 2:28,29) were being fulfilled in our young lives! What we saw was so holy and awesome that we agreed to tell no one. Not until years later did we even mention the vision again to one another. To my knowledge, I shared with no one except Eldrin and then, years later, with Ruth. However, shortly before her home-going, my mother, who became a dynamic witness for Jesus as the baptizer (after learning my experience was scriptural), asked (out of the blue!) if I remembered seeing Jesus as a child. I was astounded that she knew and that, through the years, she, too, had kept this holy secret and pondered it in her heart.

The Lord let me know it was He who had kept me from throwing my pearls before the swine by not allowing me to share this childhood vision with people who would have had no regard for holy things (Matthew 7:6). His Word served to constrain me and the vision (which came profoundly to the forefront of my mind before the baptism) was given to hold me through the dark years, until I could come into the fullness of God's power for his purposes in this final hour.

I do not profess to understand all that has happened in my life. Some things, however, are very clear. The God who called me is a holy God, a consuming fire before whom nothing unclean will stand. Regardless of what you may hear or think, God has not lost any of His holiness. It was in the presence of this thrice-holy God that the revelation related herein was received. (Praise God for the blood of Jesus!) I believe it is a dangerous thing to profess to know the Lord and continue to walk in willful sin and disobedience. God is still a jealous God (Exodus 20:5) who commands first place in our lives. If this were true only under the old covenant, Jesus would not require us to forsake all to follow Him!

It is also clear that God chooses whom He wills. Man loves to have the preeminence but it is God, alone, who will get the glory. He will not share His glory with another (Isaiah 42:8). It bears repeating, God's ways are not the ways of man. Paul writes in I Corinthians 1:26, "For ye see your calling, brethren, how that not many wise men after the flesh, not many mighty, not many noble, are called." God's holy truths are hidden from the wise and prudent and revealed unto babes (Luke 10:21). God's ways are contrary to the ways of man so "that no flesh should glory in His presence" (I Corinthians 1:29).

I will not fully understand why the Lord chose me until I see Him face to face. I only know He looked beyond my fear, inadequacy and inability and said, "I want you, I choose you, I'll use you." He delights in using the most unlikely candidate – the one who appears weak and foolish in the eyes of the world to confound the wise (I Corinthians 1:27). Yes, the right to call is reserved by God alone.

Chapter Three

THROUGH THE FIRE

*"When thou passest through the waters, I will be with thee;
and through the rivers, they shall not overflow thee: when
thou walkest through the fire, thou shalt not be burned;
neither shall the flame kindle upon thee."*

(Isaiah 43:2)

As God reserves the right to choose, He also reserves
the right to test and prove. Matthew 22:14 says that many
are called, but few are chosen. Is it possible that only a few
pass a test set before them?

There are other examples, but I love Joseph's story.
Called by God at an early age, Joseph was sold into slavery,
falsely accused and imprisoned. Some thirteen years went
by before God raised him up for His purpose (Genesis 37
and 39-50). Psalm 105:19 says "the Lord tried him." Then
we are told that Jesus, the sinless Son of God and our ultimate
example, learned obedience through things suffered
(Hebrews 5:8). Yes, even Jesus, after being baptized in the
Spirit and before public ministry, was tested and proven
(Matthew 4:1-11, Luke 4:1-13).

As I returned from heaven, the Lord showed me that
something very difficult – His baptism of fire – lay just
ahead (Matthew 3:11, Luke 3:16). Fire has to do with
cleansing, purging, sanctification...holiness. My time in
God's furnace lasted seven years – His number of perfection!
It was the prerequisite for ministry ahead – a time during
which the promise from Isaiah (above) became most
precious to my soul.

The first half of this fiery ordeal was an exceedingly bitter cup that left me struggling for the will to live. Prayer was constantly required not only for strength to write a book, but to be a helpmate to my husband as we built our own home (his life-long dream), and a mother to our daughter who entered her teens. The transition from military to civilian life had to be made at the onset with a move, change of jobs and schools. Swiftly, the cup reached its brim, and then my mother died leaving my dad, old and alone, to draw upon us heavily for ministry and support and the church to which we were led split. Before I could adjust to my mother's death, the cup ran over.

The Lord had shown me I would come off glory mountain to enter the darkest valley I had ever known. He showed me it would be one of intense suffering and persecution revolving around my teen-age son who would be used as the devil's ploy. I was instructed to finish his scrapbooks and photo albums quickly, because later there would be no heart to do them. Indeed, the pain eventually grew so deep I could not even bear to look upon his picture nor enter his room of familiar belongings.

Satan comes in at a weak point – through the gap in the hedge! Testing is designed to rid us of the dross in our lives and to strengthen areas of weakness. Testing will either make us or break us – cause us to grow better or bitter. The Lord desires that we grow strong and resilient – like fine tempered steel. As we determine to follow Jesus only, we will overcome our arch-enemy, Satan, whose sole purpose is to destroy us, and our inner man will be mightily strengthened in the process.

God promises a way of escape with every temptation (I Corinthians 10:13). My way of escape came through the Word. The heavenly visit was given to sustain me and the Psalms, for which I had been given supernatural hunger, became a lifeline of comfort and confirmation throughout the valley. The Lord had further prepared by quickly getting faith tapes into my hands. He knew just what I would need to make it through!

My life had centered around dreams of a happy, close-knit family. I had tried to be a good wife and mother and to give our children every advantage. We were actively involved in the church yet our family problems grew. During Eldrin's time in Vietnam, I felt a deep need to start devotions with our children – a step in the right direction – but I knew nothing of Satan's wiles. The devil never minds a little religion while doing his dirty work under cover!

Mitch was a strong-willed child who seemed determined to go his own way and by the time he reached his early teens I felt I hardly knew my own son. Weary, after years alone as a military wife, I expected to turn over the reigns after Eldrin's return from Vietnam but those expectations were short-lived. First Sergeant duties were demanding and, as our son's strong will turned to rebellion, our home became a rocky harbor of turmoil and unrest.

With the power of the Spirit, my eyes were opened to Satan's attempts to destroy my family and I learned how to bind and loose (Matthew 18:18). The Lord gave Joel 2:25 "I will restore to you the years that the locust hath eaten" as a promise to claim for Mitch and I was ready for blessings. I could not accept what the Lord was trying to show me. My only desire for my son was to see him on fire for Jesus and I expected a quick change especially since the Lord had shown me He would begin a work in the lives of the young people on my side of the family, and also because He had told me to witness first to my son. How I prayed, wept and sought God for a miracle to turn his life around, but the miracle never came – at least not in my timing.

It has been said that to have a child leave home in

rebellion is worse than death. I believe this is true. It is like a death that will not die. Ignoring our pleas to give college a try and to get out of his turbulent teens before marriage, Mitch left home in the heat of rebellion to join the Air Force and to be married a short time later to a girl we barely knew. Refusing Godly counsel, he sought out those who told him, in effect, "Forget your parents – it's your life to live." Indirectly, we learned of his plans.

The shock of seeing my unkempt, longhaired son on his wedding day in crisp Air Force uniform with neat, short hair was almost too much. He was cleaned up on the outside, but I longed for the transformation of the inner man. With a heart that had broken into a million pieces, I prayed for the strength to reach out with God's love. The day I had dreamed of since the birth of my first born – the joyous day when he would take a bride – had become my darkest hour. Where there had been one in rebellion, now two were joined. A wall of alienation a mile wide separated us from one another. The son lost to the world years before now seemed lost forever. Even the Lord's promise to restore seemed like bitter mockery to my ears. Yet I clung to this promise as the only light at the end of the long, dark tunnel still ahead.

The past hung with painful poignancy. When we moved, Mitch stayed behind with the job we had insisted he have while still in high school. With friends, he rented a trailer off post and, although I made it clear he have his own place after high school (knowing I could no longer take the disrespect and rebellion), I wept over his empty room. But I assured myself things would get better now – he would gain responsibility and maturity and come to appreciate family. But nothing changed. We would wait up weekends when he was expected home. Janet would bake cookies to surprise her brother only to be disappointed. He would arrive in the wee hours, or not at all. Waiting provoked anger, fear.

There were those times – the motorcycle accident, the night of the MP call (when he was picked up on the wrong side of the road with a barefoot companion too oblivious to notice the frost on the ground), the day his car was totaled and there was an urgent call for money. We were important, it seemed, only when a need arose.

As Thanksgiving neared, Mitch called to bring his new girlfriend home. I was hesitant. In spite of evidence, I refused to believe he was getting involved again after Lili. I could not believe the liberty allowed young girls. Was I back in the dark ages? After Lili, it had been especially unsettling to see the new girl's car on our street late at night. "Please, Mom," Mitch begged, "I've changed, Mom, really I've changed." How I wanted to believe!

For nearly two years, our family had simply existed in a state of constant duress as Mitchell literally sold his soul to the girl across the street. While karate, rock music and liquor vied for first place in his life (and drugs were suspected), Lili became a household word – an "albatross" around our necks! She wore his tiny diamond promise ring in an obsessive, inseparable, relationship that superseded all else. Grades dropped and notes came from teachers. Lili's mother thought the affair was "cute" – no longer did Lili walk the dog "to wind up in some guy's house." Our attempts to enforce restrictions brought offense. Praying for strength to talk to Lili alone, I stressed school, friends and other interests as Lili wept. Lacking parental support, there was only Mitchell and, knowing his strong will, marriage was inevitable. With anguished heart, I prayed that God would help me love and accept a daughter-in-law not yet sixteen.

Our young pastor (mainly concerned with our fairness) concluded after counsel, "Mitch, the monkey's on your back. Your parents are doing all in their power to be fair to you." Later, he suggested a talk with Marie whose son, with similar background, was delivered from drugs through the power of Jesus Christ. After sharing and prayer with Don and Marie, Mitch and Lili broke up. Mitch appeared to live again as friends and other interest re-entered his life and, cautiously, we breathed easier. But all too soon a new girl was on the scene and, once again, with behavioral patterns as strong as ever and still without recognizable direction, Mitch was talking marriage! I could not, *would not*, believe we were back where we started.

In spite of misgivings, my mother's heart agreed to the holiday visit and, with a spark of hope, I made preparations. Baptized in the Spirit just months before, God's holy fire burned within me. I did so want all to be right and pleasing to the Lord. But the visit proved devastating with difficult steps ordered by the Holy Ghost that left me looking like an ogre in the eyes of those for whom God held me accountable.

A disturbing call from the trailer court management convinced us to get Mitch home. He came to work with his dad, but his heart was not with us. Seeking counsel from the Spirit-filled pastor in our new location, I finally got Mitch to see him, but after one meeting he walked out of our lives. (Later, I was stunned to learn he had lied to our pastor telling him he had no time to meet). Left behind to pierce my heart like a knife was a family portrait taken shortly before Eldrin's army retirement. It had been crumpled and thrown into his trash.

Like one last defiant slap in the face, Mitch was gone. It was so abrupt, so final, like an untimely birth. With blinding indignation, I recalled childhood when our old farm dog, suddenly and viciously, without reason, attacked a pregnant cat. Her tiny kittens, violently aborted, had no chance to live. So it seemed with Mitch. There was no mellowing, no transition from child to adult, no time to reflect as one would look upon a plant growing well. I thought of the pruning needed to bear fruit (John 15:2) and wept bitter tears. Our new daughter-in-law gave no evidence of the new birth. Adding to my consternation was her membership in an organization the Lord confirmed to be demonic. "Why, Lord?" I cried. I had prayed so hard not only for my son, but also for a born-again, Spirit-filled wife.

The wedding was over but the battle had just begun. Desperately, I wanted to forget the past but excruciating reminders of "the son who was no more" were everywhere – Pontiac Firebirds like the one he drove – teen-age couples holding hands – his favorite songs before hard rock. In an uncanny way, Harry Chapin's "The Cat's in the Cradle" would crop up to haunt. How it tore at my already bleeding heart. At one point, Mitch had tried to get his message across through this ballad but his dad had been unable to decode that message. I had tried so hard to bridge the gap but I, too, had failed.

The pain cut so deeply I wanted to get out of the world but I knew I was in God's wine-press where the dictates of the flesh would be treaded out and burned away in God's holy fire. I thought of Psalm 51:10 given as I re-entered my bedroom from heaven – "Create in me a clean heart, O God; and renew a right spirit within me" – and understood clearly what the baptism of fire was all about. All earthly props fell away as I was cast in utter dependence upon the Lord. No one, not even my husband (although he hurt too), fully understood this test just for me. The misunderstanding and aloneness were most unbearable but I resolved, "though He slay me, yet will I trust in Him" (Job 13:15) – I held on to the horns of the altar! The Lord gave comfort through Isaiah 42:3 that He would not break a bruised reed and He provided a precious daughter whose sweet, gentle spirit was as the balm of Gilead to my broken heart. Ministering the Psalms when I could not even read them for myself, Janet became

God's grace extended. I simply could not have made it without her.

The most difficult aspect of this trial was not our son's behavior (difficult as it was) but a source which had greatly influenced his life through the years aiding and abetting the rebellious spirit. It joined forces with others. *A coalition had been forming in the pit of hell.* The devil, using those dismayed and angered by my witness for the Lord – those who should have been standing with us in prayerful support for our son's spiritual welfare, now found perfect occasion to rise full strength against us. With every fiber of my being, I knew I must look to the Lord, for Satan was out to destroy my joy and witness and, specifically, the book God had commissioned! We were ostracized, I was mocked and falsely accused and Janet (most needing the love and support of family), was cut off without mercy. Prayerfully confronting the issue, we were met with the hostility of those "in the seat of the scornful" (Psalm 1:1). I could almost hear the devil's "Aha, she was on the mountain with God – look at her now!"

Mind battles commanded aggressive use of the Sword and pleading the Blood (II Corinthians 10:3-5, Ephesians 6:10-17, and Revelations 12:11). In a recurring dream concerning my stand for righteousness, I awoke one night literally fighting for survival as the scorners came taunting and jeering. This battle was against principalities and powers (Ephesians 6:12)! Crying out in desperation, I opened my Bible to words that left me awestruck: "If it had not been the Lord who was on our side, *when men rose up against us*: then they had swallowed us up quick, when their wrath was kindled against us – then the proud waters had gone over our soul...blessed be the Lord, who hath not given us as prey to their teeth – our soul is escaped as a bird out of the snare of the fowlers" (Psalm 124:2,3,5-7, my emphasis).

With tears of relief and release, I praised God for His blessed way of escape!

From Psalm 124, I was led to Proverbs 30 where, again, I stared, in absolute awe: "There is a generation that curseth father and doth not bless mother – pure in own eyes yet not washed from filthiness, whose teeth are as swords - the eye that mocketh father, despiseth to obey mother - ravens shall pick it out - eagles shall eat it" (v 11-14,17)...I knew these Scriptures had not come by chance that night. The Lord had shown me rebellion was as witchcraft (I Samuel 15:23) and that a stronghold, operating from birth over my son's life, had finally overtaken completely. This was no light skirmish in spiritual warfare but an all-out struggle, not only for my own survival and the work God had called me to do, but for the eternal welfare of my son.

As an intercessor, my heart must be clean. I chose to love, forgive and pray for my enemies and to praise and thank God in the midst of the circumstances (Matthew 5:44, I Thessalonians 5:18). Over and over I heard the Lord say, "Vengeance is mine," and "I will vindicate you"! Scriptures came on how the trial of faith, more precious than gold, develops patience, perfects, establishes, strengthens, settles (I Peter 1:7, James 1:3,4, I Peter 5:10). "Lord", I thought, "surely you could have chosen a different way! It was so much easier (back) in the old church." Reminded that I had not yet suffered to the shedding of blood (Hebrews 12:4), I heard the warnings of the Holy Ghost: "No man, having put his hand to the plough, and looking back, is fit for the kingdom of God" (Luke 9:62). I remembered Lots' wife (Genesis 19:26) and the Israelites who never entered the promised land (Hebrews 3:7-19). No, I could not look back!

As a front-line soldier, I was admonished to "endure hardness as a good soldier" (II Timothy 2:3) and to set my face like a flint to carry out the Lord's commands. With the enemy everywhere, I could not freely talk about a book until the manuscript was completed. In this walk in the Spirit I saw there are no mountains without valleys, no victories without battles – no growth without pain. I saw that the flesh (which can do nothing for the glory of God) dies hard – slowly, painfully, not wanting to relinquish its "rights."

All my life I had heard "all things work together for good to them that love God" but, now, I saw the last part of Romans 8:28 – "to them who are the called *according to His purpose*" (my emphasis). I knew I loved God (with all my heart I wanted to please Him) and that I was called, but now I saw that, somehow, through this dark trial, His purpose was being carried out. From the inner peace (like the eye in the middle of the tornado!), I knew, too, that I was right in the center of God's will. Later, I saw that Romans 8 has to do with the flesh versus the spirit and that, interestingly, the two verses preceding 8:28 have to do with the infilling of the Spirit!

At times, things got so dark I felt utterly forsaken even by God and I would cry, "Lord, what (evil) have I done that I must suffer so?" I reminded the Lord I was but dust (Psalms 103:14), had no one in heaven but Him and desired nothing on earth beside Him (Psalms 73:25). How I identified with those precious Psalms! Holding on to my beginnings (knowing they had been right with the Lord), I felt like Jacob must have felt wrestling God while, from all sides, Scripture came having to do with suffering for righteousness' sake – Matthew 5:10-12, I Peter 2:19-21, I Peter 4:12-19, Romans 8:17,18, II Corinthians 4:17, II Timothy 2:12 (Unless we share in Christ's suffering we will not share in His glory). I saw that He who changes not, expects us to change – going from glory to glory conforming to His image (II Corinthians 3:18, Romans 8:29).

There were times when I could not pray for myself and

I would call Betty, a Spirit-filled friend who had known similar heartache, and her precious love and compassionate heart helped to see me through. I learned that God will provide someone in our time of need or He will simply say, "My grace is sufficient – my strength is made perfect in weakness" (II Corinthians 12:9). In the spring of 1979 Betty gave me the book, *Come Away My Beloved*, by Frances J. Roberts and, for the next several years, my time in this anointed devotional became nothing less than God-appointed.

Eventually, I understood that because I had offered myself up to follow the Lord regardless of cost, I was going the way of the cross. Often, I had cried out for a deeper understanding and appreciation of Jesus' suffering and death. Gabi had had a heart-rending vision of the crucifixion and I had something like that in mind. But one day, while watching a discussion of the crucifixion on Christian TV, the Lord spoke profoundly, *"This is the cross – the persecution you are suffering for my sake is the cross!"* I wept as this truth sank in.

Then, an excellent teaching, by Judson Cornwall on the price of the cross (Psalm 22), confirmed to the letter what the Lord was trying to show me. I'm not sure anyone else saw it, but the Lord made sure I saw this same TV program *a second day*! I saw that when we go the way of the cross, like Jesus, we will not get a fair deal. The scorners will be present to take the glory flow, if possible, and God will separate His conscious presence from us. We'll wonder why He is dealing with us in such a way. But there was the promise of resurrection life on the other side of the cross as well as the assurance that those who have been placed under (God's) authority will be placed in authority.

The Lord quickened two Scriptures that brought much comfort by assuring me I was not suffering for some sin in my life. The Word declares in I Peter 4:1 that those who suffer in the flesh (armed with the mind of Christ) have ceased from sin! Even more profound, Colossians 1:24 let me know I was filling up that which was behind of the sufferings of Christ for the sake of His body, the Church. WOW! I didn't even know such a verse existed! This was quickly confirmed through *Come Away My Beloved* and, later, seeing my place in the body of Christ, I understood fully. When we suffer for well doing and take it patiently, it is acceptable to God (I Peter 2:20). Anything can be endured if we know we are in God's perfect will and pleasing Him!

In a test of faith it is vitally important to remember God's great love for us and His promise never to forsake us (Hebrews 13:5). Romans 8:28 *is* being carried out! Can God trust us with such a test? Will we walk in the flesh or in the Spirit (Galatians 5:19-23) trusting Him for vindication in due time? In His righteousness, He must deal with our persecutors (II Thessalonians 1:6). We must endure with patience (standing on the Word) as we crucify the flesh and firmly resist the devil.

As I stood in the gap binding, weeping, praying, "Lord, save the son of thy handmaid" (Psalm 86:16), I prayed also for his wife (they were one) and for her family whom the Lord promised through Psalm 2:8 if I would ask! Was this part of the larger picture of Romans 8:28?

I knew the Lord's promised vindication would come with book publication and a turn-around in the life of my son. As I walked through the fire, however, I wondered how either of these miracles (and, indeed they would be miracles!) would ever come to pass.

Toward the end of 1979, a call from Mitch back in the States from Germany, confirmed a word of knowledge given just days before through a visiting minister. There was no way of knowing the test was only half over but, with a taste of vindication, I began my way up out of the long, dark valley.

Chapter Four

SIGNS AND WONDERS

"And these signs shall follow those that believe; in my name shall they cast out devils; they shall speak with new tongues; they shall take up serpents; and if they drink any deadly thing, it shall not hurt them; they shall lay hands on the sick, and they shall recover."

(Mark 16:17,18)

Jesus said signs would follow those who believe (Mark 16:17,18) and, indeed, they do! The next two chapters can only highlight a few of the ways in which the Lord manifested Himself throughout the fire and beyond.

One of the first signs witnessed in our new location was God's plan of multiplication through division. Since light and darkness will not dwell together, it was no surprise when the church to which we were led, split. Synod "reviewed" the case and the "scribes" and "Pharisees" worked overtime to get rid of the Holy Ghost. One person (not a member), who attended a meeting, described our pastor's treatment: "My God! It was as though they were crucifying our Lord!" Pastor Birdsong was voted out and he, the elders and half the congregation had to find a new home (What the Lord had revealed was coming to pass to the letter!). How blessed we felt, after renting for two years, when Golgotha Lutheran Church was dedicated, with the unmistakable presence of the Holy Spirit in our midst, excitement ran high. We wondered what great work the Lord had in store!

The counsel of a Spirit-filled Pastor was greatly valued as the dregs in the cup grew exceedingly bitter and corresponding with our son and his wife finally became impossible. When we received a "family" magazine article condoning teen "freedom" telling parents, in effect, to keep out, Pastor Birdsong was quick to supply Scriptures refuting that article. Later, when "Scripture-based" material came that subtly attacked the new birth; he confirmed the literature, being distributed by our daughter-in-law at her work place, was from a cult. Our precious children seemed to be willing prey for the devil's snares and ambassadors for his cause!

Getting cult material was like the last straw and, once again, I found myself imploring the Lord, with all my heart, for wisdom. Strongly, Revelation 19:20 came to mind, which speaks of the false prophet (and those he deceives) who will be "cast alive into the lake of fire." I wrote back identifying the material as that of a cult and included this Scripture. It was tough love I knew would not be received, but I was not prepared for my son's scathing rebuttal! Out of love, I thought I must reply, but try as I might, I could not. Then one day as I sat with pen in hand, it was as though the hand of God came down over mine. Ever so gently, He spoke, "You have done enough, you will do no more." Peace flooded my battle-weary soul. It seemed I could hear the final clashing of swords in a mop-up operation in the heavenlies. Surely, the battle for my son was clinched! Later, I realized, that even before this incident, the prayer burden had lifted.

In September, Mitch wrote in my birthday card a note: "Mother, what has come between us is a difference of opinion; I pray it might be resolved." In his birthday card in November, the Lord allowed a brief response: "Mitch, what has come between us is not a difference of opinion but a Person – His Name is Jesus Christ. We, and others who know His love and forgiveness, are praying for you."

It was Friday, November 30, 1979. Cover Church was starting a retreat at Golgotha and I felt I must go. I had no transportation, but the Lord made sure I got there by having Betty call and insist on picking me up! That evening, through brother Onn, this word came forth: "There is a mother here who has suffered much anguish because of her son – the Lord would have you know your prayers have not been in vain for in two or three days you will see such a change in your son as you will not be able to believe." Betty squeezed my hand as I backed away from the altar with tears streaming down. I knew this word was for me yet it seemed too good to be true. "Betty," I said, "Do I dare claim that word?" With tears of joy, Betty confirmed, "Chris, that word was for you!"

The excitement was too much to contain as the Lord began to show me Mitch and Mary were back in the States from Germany. There had been no real communication for months and we did not expect them home until later, but I *knew I* was hearing from the Lord. The weekend passed and the expectation grew. On Tuesday morning I said, "Now, Lord, if that word was really for me from you, You must do something soon. It has been three days."

A short while later, the phone rang. It was Mitch calling from Mary's parents! His voice had changed and deepened into manhood. I told him his call was no surprise because of the word from the Lord concerning him. After a silence, he asked if the word was good or bad! I said good but nothing more till years later. As we talked his words hit home "Mom, I *felt* your prayers!" He shared how, at times working with electrical systems, his life had been endangered. He also shared how two Mormons tried hard to "convert" him (and he was interested) but, always, waiting in the wings, was this laborer who would step in after they left, open his Bible and say, "Now, Mitch, listen to me, that's not the way it is!"

Mitchell exclaimed, "Mom, he sounded just like you! (Consistently, I had prayed for laborers across his path)." When I got off the phone, it hit me. The spirit of rebellion was gone! Only then could the Lord begin a work in his life. And, while this was, indeed, a glorious change – one I could hardly believe, I knew it was only the beginning of the turnaround. I would hold onto God for that deeper work in his life.

The Lord was granting the desires of my heart. That August, under Bill Banks' ministry at a full Gospel meeting, Eldrin received the baptism in the Holy Spirit and, later, after a glory-filled camp meeting, he returned on fire for Jesus with Scriptures written all over the inside covers of his Bible. He has testified that, although a church elder, he was lost and on his way to hell before my own encounter with the Lord. In time, he became an officer in the local Men's Full gospel Businessmen's chapter and a vibrant ambassador for Jesus through that organization.

While waiting for the Lord to move in the young people on my side of the family, I began to wonder if I had really heard from the Lord. Then, in the summer of 1980, my seventeen-year-old niece, Sherry, was gloriously saved. She was given graphic illustrations – one of how Satan blinds us (in a tunnel with rose-colored glasses on thinking all is O.K.!) before our eyes are opened to salvation. There is no greater miracle than salvation! Never have I seen anyone so hungry for the things of the Lord as Sherry. What a blessed privilege it was to minister as she soaked up the Word like a sponge. Deeply touched when she heard singing in tongues at Golgotha the following summer, she later received this blessed gift. Later, her sister Tammy, reading *There's More to be Had* while away at college was also deeply touched by the Lord.

The next summer, during a situation the devil intended

for evil, Janet received. Returning home late one night bone tired and weary from one of our many mercy missions (where oppression was unusually heavy), strife came between Eldrin and me. Janet had gone to bed but got up to mediate and lovingly tried to minister but soon realized her own inadequacy. Crying out to the Lord, she began to sing over me *in a beautiful heavenly tongue*! Desiring the baptism, she was afraid she would not receive. Now, forgetting herself in concern for me, the Lord broke through to touch her and me where nothing else could have touched me at the time. The Holy Ghost knows how to pray! Oppression vanished as I melted under the Lord's precious goodness.

The Lord had previously given me a "sign" of how tongues come from the spirit, not the head. Trying to get beyond my first syllables, I knew I must again step out on faith (like Peter walking on water), but my head got in the way. I was stuck and it was humorous. I would go "a sticky a, a sticky a," over and over! I kept calling on the Lord for help and then Eldrin astounded me by saying I was praying in tongues through the night. I did not believe him, thinking he was trying to make me feel good. Then, one night I woke myself up praying in tongues! Tongues are a sign, I Corinthians 14:22 says, to those who believe not! What a precious sense of humor the Lord has. When our heads get out of the way, our spirits have no trouble communing with God.

Romans 8:26 says that the Spirit helps us when we don't know how to pray as we ought. Prayer in the Spirit is the perfect will of God. In the emergency room, where Eldrin was given morphine for pain and surgery was pending after a third major kidney stone attack, I simply could not have made it without tongues. With hands laid upon my ash-gray husband, I prayed in the Spirit. If someone entered, I would sit down and pray quietly in the Spirit. When a nurse emphasized that one never gets past a second attack without surgery (relating her own husband's surgery after a second attack), I was sure Satan had sent her to erode my faith! But, I never stopped praying in tongues.

It was especially difficult to tell Janet early that morning that we were leaving for the hospital knowing she would be alone to get up later to meet the bus for school. We had to lean heavily upon each other and the Lord and, although she often carried responsibility beyond her years, it was never easy to leave her. In the midst of the fire and at the end of my rope, I told the Lord he would have to carry me all the way should surgery be necessary.

Finally, in early afternoon, Eldrin was wheeled into the hall for preliminaries before surgery. Exhausted, I sat watching from the emergency room door when he suddenly sat bolt upright on the stretchers declaring he was better and ready to go home! After observation he was released and we knew we were spared surgery during a most difficult time through a miracle of God's intervention. Glory!

At another time, praying Mark 16:17,18 for my dad (near pneumonia), we felt a release of God's power. Planning hospitalization, his doctor verified the next day that his lungs were clear. With a prayer of thanks, I testified in church and obeyed the Lord by writing a letter of testimony to my sister, Darline. Before these steps were taken, however, I began to feel heaviness in my spirit and the Lord showed me that the devil was going to try to rob me of my testimony and that I must stand fast! The letter had hardly reached its destination before my dad, seemingly worse, was hospitalized. I held onto the testimony of healing and, while tests were run, nothing significant was found and my dad was released. Again, glory to God!

Jesus is also our deliverer. When Janet, who was

asthmatic, was hit full force by an attack soon after I received God's power, I had to learn quickly how to engage in spiritual combat in a vulnerable area. Gabi tore away the devils' curtain by stating, emphatically, that asthma was demonic. Then, revelation came through Exodus 20:5 that this debilitating disease came via the curse of the generations and needed to be renounced and broken off. Our ancestors dabbled in that which the Lord forbids (see Deuteronomy 18:10-13). Through ignorance of the Word (Hosea 4:6), many have perished. Jesus became a curse for us (Galatians 3:13) so we don't have to be under a curse! The devil held on with tenacity but, praise God, the truth set us free. Janet became a normal, healthy teenager fulfilling her love of competitive sports by acquiring honors in that field both in high school and college.

One day, while preoccupied in the depths of the valley, I witnessed, dramatically, the mighty power in the name of Jesus in an emergency situation. Going maximum speed in heavy homebound traffic to pick up Janet after Jr. High band practice, I failed to see the right turn signal of the car up ahead. With no time to stop, a right turn would have meant a pile-up. Beyond that, there was no time to think. Braking, calling out JESUS!, and veering to the left (across oncoming traffic!) all at the same time, I found myself safely parallel parked on the shoulder on the opposite side of the highway! Momentarily stunned, as the traffic swished by, I could not understand why I was headed in the opposite direction or why I was untouched. It did not take long, however, to comprehend that, simply by calling on the name of Jesus, the Lord had completely overtaken to spare me from what surely would have been a very serious accident.

Some time after this incident, four young people from Rhema Bible School in Tulsa, Oklahoma spoke at Golgotha. En route, their car was demolished in a head-on collision.

They were able to walk away from the accident. Although their pale appearance (and aching bodies) gave mute testimony to the close brush with death, they bubbled with joy in their witness. They shared how, after assisting one another and checking on the other driver, they discovered that each had uttered the same Word a split second before impact – *Jesus*! Needless to say, their testimony had special meaning for me.

Often, we have seen the Lord move in practical ways. Since He tells us to put Him in remembrance of His Word (Isaiah 43:26), we have used Matthew 10:26 to remind Him that hidden things will be revealed and have been directed to lost articles in astounding ways. Once, after learning of Eldrin's lengthy search for a misplaced rifle magazine clip, I suggested we pray, reminding the Lord of his word. Within seconds, hallelujahs erupted from the next room when Eldrin pulled back the curtain to view the weather. There on the window ledge behind the curtain, lay the missing clip!

Another instance came after one of Janet's bridal showers when we stopped to fit Sherry's dress before she left town. We were anxious to head home after a long day, but Janet could not find her car keys. As the girls retraced their steps, I knelt reminding the Lord of His Word (aloud for both myself and my sister, Iona, in the car). Returning, Janet emptied her purse again and we heard the rattle of keys! Hidden between purse and lining, they had fallen through a rip in the lining seam. Only the Lord could have known they were there. I had a hallelujah meeting in the parking lot! What a wonderful God we serve who sees what we cannot see and cares about every detail of our lives.

In yet another remarkable way, the Lord manifested his power while we visited a friend after her husband's funeral. As we prayed quietly before leaving, the house (filled with a party spirit of smoking, drinking and card playing) got stone quiet as all eyes focused upon us. A weighty silence prevailed before we were introduced around the table in the adjoining room. We knew we could not be heard so it was obvious that the Lord, for His own divine purpose, had turned up the volume on our prayer! We have since heard similar testimonies.

On one occasion I was prompted to put on praise music before a young lady brought out photo coupons I had been led to purchase by phone. Just inside the front door she stopped short to exclaim, "That's my favorite song!" Of all our praise songs, her favorite "happened" to be on. We had a blessed time of sharing and I thought that was the end of the story but there was more to come.

Praying that we would not buy unwisely, we did not reckon on super saleslady, Cara! Before we knew it, we had purchased an expensive wall "canvas." Unhappy with what we felt was high pressure and a bad attitude, we considered contacting customer relations but were glad we did not (our purchase eased sales pressure and paved the way for the Lord later). Our next proof viewing was rescheduled because Cara, who came in briefly to help out, was sick. The photographer said she might need to be hospitalized and, as Cara turned to look up, I was sure I had never seen anyone who looked so deathly ill.

That evening Cara weighed on my mind. Struggling with my feelings and the devil's lie that she had died, I finally awakened Eldrin since the prompting to pray (with him) for Cara was so strong. Asking forgiveness for ill feelings, I said, "Lord, I do not think Cara knows you but she needs prayer. If she doesn't know you, please save her and heal her." That night I dreamed we were in a booth with Cara opposite (as in the viewing booth) when, after a few words, Cara looked up at me and said, "Oh, I am a child of God!" It did not seem possible, but soon I would know this was a

God-given dream.

The next day, taking salvation tracts and a booklet, *My World Was Caving In*, to which I felt a strong leading, I came under a heavy, unexplainable attack which I knew had to do with the Lord's business that evening! Eldrin stood with me against the powers of darkness and, later, I found myself reaching for the booklet as I told Cara I had prayed for her healing. She thanked me saying she had never been so sick (with flu) in her life, glanced at the booklet (admitting things could be better), then looked up and said, "Oh, I am a child of God"! I told her about the dream and the power of God fell in that place that evening! Since Eldrin knew about the dream but nothing of my intention to witness, he, too, was tremendously blessed.

Much prayer went up for Cara who later confided that her husband was an alcoholic. The booklet I was led to give was written by an alcoholic set free by Jesus! With each contact after our blessed encounter, Cara greeted us with a glowing smile. Her whole countenance changed as well as her physical appearance (through needed weight loss) as she gained new strength in the Lord. A "canvas" hangs in our home as a memorial to God's sovereign ways!

Another dream gave a "sneak preview" of my daughter's future profession. This dream (unlike any I've had), brief, graphic and in living color, featured Janet in full nursing regalia on a major Christian university campus. Doors opened in high school and a nursing scholarship followed, but my dream was all but forgotten as she went another direction. Not until after a college P.E. degree and marriage did she attend nursing school persuaded by her husband, Jack, who knew nothing of my dream! She is now a bona fide nurse with the second part of the dream yet to be fulfilled.

Once, I was made aware of what was surely the presence

of angels when sisters in the Lord who had just arrived from out of town went into a state of ecstasy over an extraordinary fragrance – "like loads of freshly cut pine boughs" – just inside the front door. Puzzled, because we had nothing around with a pine scent, I excused myself to go upstairs for something and, as I returned, I, too, was given a glorious whiff. Later, I recalled testimonies about the fragrance of angels and knew we must have had a heavenly visitation that day!

Occult involvement was uncovered on one occasion after Eldrin gave a copy of my book to a Christian co-worker who called me. We had a God-appointed time of sharing, but when I got off the phone the impression grew that I must call back to tell her to renounce occult activity! After a long silence, when I told her what I felt the Lord was showing me, she quietly reflected out loud, "But it was so long ago." She had dabbled in witchcraft in Jr. High even painting her fingernails black to emulate the craft! If I recall, she had also played the Ouija board. This involvement (probably the source of many problems in her life) was keeping her from the power of God. Through God's infinite wisdom, the devil's dark secrets were uncovered.

At another time, the Lord chose to uncover fornication in a way that left me particularly disdained by the one exposed. At a Bible study on Proverbs 7, I found myself stressing a portion over and over not knowing why I was doing so. Later, a scathing letter came from one who had attended. In the process of attempting justification, this person's sin was disclosed, which till then, I knew nothing of! Numbers 32:23 says, "your sin will find you out"!

Perhaps the most dramatic incident involved our poodle, Sam. Before Janet (then 16) left for her first basketball camp, I tried to dismiss a premonition as mother's qualms since she would be out of state on her own. But when she expressed the same foreboding, I got concerned. Psalm 91 came to mind. At the time I knew only that this powerful Psalm said something about the Lord covering us with His feathers but as I read down, verses 9-11 were quickened. Verse 11, "He shall give His angels charge over thee in all thy ways," was for Janet while away and verse 10, "neither shall any plague come nigh thy dwelling," covered us at home. I copied the verses for Janet to take with her and then tried to rest in the Lord.

One morning later, hearing a constant "yip, yip" which I thought to be a new puppy next door, the Holy Spirit suddenly gave urgency that Sam, left on the deck, was in trouble. Racing to his aid, I found him on his back with chain collar twisted tightly between the deck boards. He was choking to death! My mind raced frantically! If only Eldrin were home – but even a cutting tool would take too long. Grabbing a table knife, I worked for what seemed like an eternity before the chain was pried loose. In the meantime, Sam had gone limp. He had lost control of his faculties. His eyes were glazed and fixed and I sensed the presence of a death which I would not accept.

The devil spoke, "Sam's dead, how will you tell Janet?" Then, "Where will you bury him?" Weeping and crying out to the Lord as I held the limp dog up before me, Psalm 91:10 came to my remembrance! Holding onto this promise, I said, "Sam, you will live, in the Name of Jesus!" Again, it seemed like an eternity with nothing happening when the Lord spoke, "You have a heavenly language. Use it!" Unmindful of the neighbors as I prayed loudly in tongues, I felt little quivers of life returning to Sam's body! Satan spoke a third time, "Even if you pray this dog back to life, he will be a vegetable from brain damage." I knew there was every possibility of brain damage, but Satan had already lost a victory. Sam responded and soon regained his ability to walk.

(Scar tissue would remain on the surface of one eye as a testimony to this incident.) I was having a Holy Ghost camp meeting when the Lord spoke, "I've done a miracle here. I want you to testify in church Sunday"!

Pastor Birdsong had asked me several weeks earlier to testify but I was "waiting on the Lord." Fear of speaking before people got in the way. If our spirits are willing (even though our flesh is weak), the Lord will assist us in obedience even through the resurrection of a dog! That Sunday "happened" to be one allowing for testimony. With church packed and in progress, I glanced at my bulletin just in time to see "A time to testify"! As this was announced, Eldrin nudged, "You need to get up!" I had not told him I was to testify *that* Sunday. After two other testimonies, with heart pounding, I got up. Satan was making in-roads at Golgotha and there was much, in addition to Sam, to which the Lord wanted me to testify. He would have to supply the courage and put it all together. He did in a beautiful way.

Not only did I share the incident concerning Sam, but I also testified about the Baptism in the Holy Spirit (with the evidence of speaking in tongues), receiving God's power, being taken to heaven, etc. People were blessed. Later, I decided to get a tape for my Dad. But when Eldrin approached the person in charge of the tapes, his face turned beet red. We got the tape all right but my testimony had been cut completely out!

Chapter Five

INTERCESSION, A HIGH AND HOLY CALLING

"And I sought for a man among them, that should make up the hedge, and stand in the gap before me for the land, that I should not destroy it: but I found none."
(Ezekiel 22:30)

I do not believe it is possible to separate signs and wonders from intercession. The two go together. It has been said that God does nothing apart from prayer and that when He moves, someone, somewhere, has been praying. What an awesome thought! God looks for those who will stand in the gap and pray. Through intercession, battles are won, tragedies are averted, revivals are born, souls are birthed into the kingdom of God, and the list goes on and on. Through intercession, ministries are birthed and we find our place in the body of Christ. Only heaven will reveal the magnitude of the vital ministry of intercession which, I believe, God wants to keenly develop, first and foremost, in the body of Christ in these latter days. Every believer is called to take his position at the post of prayer. Satan fears nothing more.

The intercessor's requirements are simple. First, there must be a loving, compassionate heart that is yielded to the Lord. It is through the agape love of God "shed abroad in our hearts by the Holy Ghost" (Romans 5:5), that we get into the yoke with Jesus to literally become one with those for whom we intercede. The intercessor's heart must also be clean before God (Psalms 24:3,4, Psalms 66:18; and

Psalms 139:23, 24). And, since he will be given insight into the spiritual realm, he must be able to keep God's secrets sharing only when, and if, God gives the liberty to share (Luke 2:19; 9:36). Finally, there must be a willingness to carry out the difficult assignments that may be given while in the closet of prayer.

Coming into the things of the Lord not only gave me a fervent desire to pray, but a strong inner witness that someone back in my ancestry – someone I never knew – had prayed for me. I felt the power of those prayers in my spirit. You may ask, how can this be? I do not know, but I look forward with great anticipation to meeting that person in heaven one day. Sometimes the Lord lets us know how we are used in intercession. Other times, He does not. The greatest blessings I've known have come as a result of being available to pray. Had there been no other assignment, I would have been content as an intercessor. It is a high and holy calling.

Twice, that I am aware of, lives have been spared from tragic endings as a result of intercession. A few months after the baptism, I was given what I thought to be a prayer burden for my sister-in-law, Suzuko (Sue) preparing to visit her native Japan. But after she left, the burden intensified and settled over her household and I knew that the grave danger I was sensing had to do with her family. Two weeks later, her teenage son was critically injured, but miraculously spared, in a serious car accident. With the news of the accident, I realized the burden had lifted and I knew exactly why I had been called to pray. This was my first such experience and what a blessed, exciting experience it was! My nephew, David, is alive and well today as a result of the Lord's saving power through intercession.

The second incident involved a sister in the Lord who came before me while in prayer. After fifteen minutes of intense intercession, the burden lifted and I knew her need had been met. I asked the Lord to let me see her at church that Sunday if He wanted me to have details. When our eyes met that Sunday, it was as though she wanted to avoid me or to run. She loved the Lord with all her heart and I was shown that her action was the result of demonic oppression. Pressing in, knowing my steps were ordered of the Lord, I soon had her full attention. Bursting into tears when she learned the time of the burden, she said she had left her husband and children. (The devil had convinced her they would be better off without her.) During the exact time of my burden her mind was changed and she returned home. This was reason enough to rejoice, but later she told the rest of the story. Not only had she left home, but, with a rope around her neck, she was ready to hang herself! Praise the Lord forevermore for thwarting the devil's plans!

On several occasions, the Lord's hand of mercy has extended to neighbors. One lady, for whom I had been burdened to pray, but had never met, moved out of a heart-rending divorce/re-marriage situation into the next duplex. The Lord not only put her on my heart, but on my doorstep! Her husband had been attracted to a younger woman and Rita, despondent and bitter after the break-up, had lost everything she ever cared about, including her children. The one thing she held on to was her job. In the midst of my own difficult circumstances, I tried to reach out with Jesus' love.

One night, returning home late from a mercy mission, we found our street flashing with police car lights. Knowing, instinctively, that Rita was involved, I cried, "Dear God, don't let her be dead or dying!" As we pulled up, the police came running to get the master key from Eldrin who worked at the time for the apartment owner. (The Lord had our arrival timed perfectly!) They had been trying to get into

Rita's apartment after receiving a call from a family member who could not get Rita to answer her phone or door. Checking in on Janet (who had stayed to do homework and was waiting up for our return), I told Eldrin to wait for me before unlocking Rita's door.

With concern only for Rita, I headed up the stairs to her bedroom when the police blocked my way. Trying to wait on the Lord, I lost all restraint when Rita's screams pierced the night and all havoc broke loose from the upper chambers. Rita had taken pills to sleep and to block out unwanted interference that Sunday when suddenly startled by the police in her bedroom who were there, not only to check on her welfare, but, evidently, at family request, to take her in. On top of her bed, yelling and screaming, Rita let it be known, in no uncertain terms, that it was not her wish to be taken in! Dresser pieces, broken in anger, were strewn about the floor.

Entering this scene, I said to the police, quietly, but authoritatively, "Will you please just leave?" That wasn't me! Without a word, they left the room. The Lord was in control of this situation. For the next hour or so, I forgot all else trying to minister God's love to Rita. Her main concern was what the neighbors would think (after all the commotion) and how she would face them going to work the next morning.

Rejoining Eldrin and the police at the foot of the stairs later, I realized the biggest hurdle was still ahead. Once before during the family breakup, Rita had been hospitalized with stress. In my spirit, I knew if they took her in that night she would never again be a free woman. The lady in uniform seemed to know a bit too much about everything, but the man lent a sympathetic ear. Listening quietly and reflectively as I pled Rita's case, he finally asked if we would be responsible if Rita took her life that night!

Eldrin answered with an emphatic, "She's not going to take her life!" And, with that, the police left. The word of a disgruntled policewoman wafted back, "You can bet on it, we'll be back tonight!" Praise God, she was wrong. We talked and prayed with Rita, and Eldrin promised to call and awaken her when he got up for work a few hours later. I stayed even longer. There was little sleep for any of us that night, but Rita got over the biggest hurdle she probably ever had to face. She made it to work the next morning and the devil lost another victory!

Through my Bible study group, I learned of another wife and mother on our street who really needed prayer. Kay was suicidal. I prayed for her for perhaps a year and then met her shortly before she moved, when she came to borrow the master key. I knew it was the Lord who had sent her to my door and He prompted me to tell her I had been praying for her. We talked for an hour or so about spiritual things and, later, through an interesting set of circumstances and a word of knowledge, the Lord manifested his all-knowing power to Kay in a way that left us both astounded.

About the time I met Kay, I was also involved with a teenager I will call Sally. Sally, whom we knew from the church in our previous location, was hospitalized with grand mal seizures at the mental health center in our area. One day she called (as she did quite often) to say that her roommate, with "lots of problems," was "really getting to her." Out of the blue, I asked for her roommate's name and promised to pray for Melinda. Sometime later, Kay came again to borrow the key. Almost immediately, she began to express concern for her "little" sister. As she did, the Holy Spirit came all over me. "Kay," I said, "Is your sister's name Melinda?" Incredulously, she answered "Yes! How did you know?" I told her how the Lord had just shown me that Sally's roommate, for whom I had been praying, was her sister. There was no way, in the natural to know this since I knew nothing of Kay's background.

The door had swung open for ministry and, as Kay and I talked, more drama unfolded. Recently, Kay had met the former owner of the house she and her husband bought in the city. In shocked amazement, he had told Kay she looked exactly like his (deceased) wife who, shortly before, had taken her life in that house! "Kay," I exclaimed, "the Lord is trying to tell you something! The devil is out to destroy you and your family and the Lord has sent you here!" Warfare ministry followed and I strongly exhorted Kay to get into a Spirit-led church as quickly as possible after her move. Prayer continued for Kay and, although I lost contact, I believe the Lord began a work in her life that day that foiled the devil's evil schemes. Through intercession, the door had opened for ministry to both Rita and Kay.

Other precious testimonies come to mind to show how God uses intercession as groundwork for deliverance. Once, a young lady confronted me in concern for her brother, a believer, who had asked for the baptism in the Holy Spirit, but had not received. As the three of us talked, I said I didn't know what, but there might be a blockage. Sometime later, a strong intercessory burden (which I knew had to do with deliverance) came upon me for this young man that lasted for two weeks. Later, I learned that, during this time, a terrible battle with alcohol ensued (I knew nothing of this problem) and he was led to people who ministered deliverance. Set free, then filled with the Spirit, he became a totally changed person on fire for the Lord!

Another testimony involved a brother in the Lord (a bleeding sheep placed on my heart) for whom prayer went up almost continuously. With "three strikes" against him (you name it, he had been through it), he hungered and thirsted for "more" of God. Jesus set him free from alcohol (and their meetings!) and then from a medication upon which he had been dependant. But there was a spirit of fear (from the past) that would, at times, take him over. One day, this fear came upon him while driving and he stopped to call. It was my first time to bind the spirit of fear out loud with someone (and it was not easy to do) but, later, he said that had it not been for that ministry at that time he knew he would have been back in the hospital again for an indefinite stay. Praise God!! He was later filled with the Spirit and became a powerful witness for the Lord. The countless hours of prayer and ministry became reciprocal when he was used of the Lord, through tapes and other ministry materials, to mightily confirm along the way what the Lord had already been showing me.

There have been many other blessings of a less dramatic nature. One involved a Golgotha elder. While praying one day, this elder and his wife came to mind and the Lord kept me in prayer for them for an hour. This was not travailing prayer but prayer on their behalf for a set time for some specific purpose. That Sunday I mentioned the prayer to the elder. He had questions concerning details then stated that, at precisely the time I was in prayer, they were listening to a tape en route to relatives that they were not particularly interested in and kept wanting to turn off, but didn't. They were amazed, later, when the Lord used the entire content of the tape to minister to, and field questions from, relatives. Glory to God!

Throughout one week, prayer went up for a sister in the Lord who came to mind constantly. She wept with surprised gratitude when I shared later saying the entire week had been one terrific struggle in her battle to lose weight. I didn't even know she was on a diet! The Lord cares about our every need and the prayers of the saints sustain and strengthen us when we feel we are going down in the battle.

In addition to putting hurting, needy people on my heart, the Lord also gave a special burden for leadership in the church. In many ways our new location had been like a desert land and I started crying out for ministers like Gabi. (After Gabi, I knew that deliverance was a valid, needed ministry in the body of Christ.) Several months later, a lady from another church, invited me to a prayer meeting. There was immediate witness when she mentioned that a sister into deliverance attended the meetings. As I waited upon the Lord at the next meeting, he confirmed that Ginny, like Gabi, was one of His special ministers. Ginny and her husband, Carl, were in a deliverance ministry together. They simply waited on the Lord to send people to their door. I greatly respected their walk in the Spirit.

Since the Lord had already shown me that, eventually, I would receive deeper ministry, I knew that meeting Ginny was no coincidence. We were put together for God's special purpose for a period of time. (More on this later) As we are sometimes prone to do, I placed Ginny far above me, spiritually, never dreaming that the Lord would choose to use me also during a time of need in her life.

One day while praying, the Lord put Ginny strongly on my heart and prompted a call asking if she had need for prayer. "Oh, Carl and I can always use prayer," she answered, nonchalantly, relating problems in their secular job. The Lord showed me she was covering up and I asked if there were something else. Hesitating, she agreed there was something else – some very bothersome persecution. Then, without fully realizing that the Holy Spirit was using me to zero in, I heard these words come out of my mouth, "Is this persecution coming from other Christians?" "Yes!" she exclaimed in astonishment as she wept almost uncontrollably with blessed Holy Ghost release.

Later, I learned that Sunny, who had also been burdened

for Ginny, was at Ginny's when I called. Sunny and I would come together at Golgotha, look at one another and, without a word, simply weep in intercession for Ginny. We had been praying for Ginny for some time before the Lord prompted my call that afternoon. As I ministered to Ginny on the phone – binding Satan's power to torment – Sunny ministered on the other end via loving touch and compassion. The Lord used the two of us to bring release to Ginny at a time when she desperately needed ministry from the body of Christ but did not know where to turn. (How we need to pray for those God has placed in leadership positions!) Later, I learned that a brother in the Lord had also been burdened to pray for Ginny. (The Lord will use those who are available.)

The burden for Ginny lifted, but then returned heavier than ever. The battle was not over. I knew that Ginny was going through a very difficult time. She was continually on my heart and in my prayers, and, eventually, I was led to call her again. At a prayer meeting several months before, she had a vision, which came forth after birth-like pangs of travail. In the vision she saw a brilliant gold ball, surrounded by purple, zooming down out of heaven upon the pores of the flesh that became greatly magnified. The Lord had given me the interpretation at that time, but I had not been led to share. He showed me that the gold ball, surrounded by purple, represented His holy, royal Kingship and that the magnified pores represented the flesh which would rise up in full strength during a time of testing and would have to die. Sensing a holy "heaviness," I knew that a time of testing lay ahead for either Ginny or myself. I was already in the fire and silently prayed, "Lord, I don't want this to be for Ginny, but please don't let it be for me!"

Reminding Ginny of this vision, I shared the interpretation which I now knew represented the time of testing she was in. For over an hour I tried to minister but she did not receive. There was a coldness about her. She desired only the Lord. She could not understand. Talking to her became more and more difficult and, finally, *my voice separated itself from me and came from across the room*! At that point, I knew I must get off the phone and pray! With great concern, I went before the Lord. Ginny, whose whole life was the Word, was now expressing *disbelief in the Word!* What was going on? Crying out to the Lord, I told Him I did not understand why Ginny could not believe the Word, but that I wanted to stand in her stead believing the Word for her, until she could again believe it for herself. This was not a heroic act on my part. The Lord knew I meant it with all my heart. (When Ginny learned of this prayer through Sunny later, she was deeply touched. The intercessor takes the place of another.)

The Lord gave spiritual insight. My voice, which had separated itself from me, represented the spirit of alienation, which had attached itself to Ginny causing her to be separated, as it were, from both the Lord and from others in the body of Christ! Needless to say, intercession continued and, eventually, Ginny emerged victorious. In a beautiful note, she expressed appreciation for ministry received, saying she honestly did not believe she could have trusted another person at the time. It is God who puts us together and burdens us for one another and it is to Him we give the glory!

Another precious saint the Lord sent across my path was Ariel. Ariel, who served for a number of years as a personal minister and intercessor for the late Kathryn Kuhlman so mightily used of God, was sent to Golgotha for a short time for a specific purpose (more later). Ever ready to do the Lord's bidding and to minister His grace, I considered her as one "in whom there was no guile." Again, I could not imagine the Lord using me to minister to Ariel but He did.

Praying for Ariel, who had come to an impasse in her life and was diligently seeking the Lord for direction, I was led to write a letter including *"Seven things to do to Help Your Ministry Grow"* by John Osteen. Through this letter with its seven points, the Lord touched Ariel as only one who knows and loves the Lord can be touched. Special ministry came through two points – Be faithful in the silent years when nobody seems to notice you and the dream seems forgotten" and, "God will bring a breakthrough." While reading my letter, the Lord gave Ariel this beautiful poem which she dedicated to me:

I Have Met the Master

I have met the Master
He's the only one of His kind.
His precious Name is Jesus
And I know He's really mine.
He has always been faithful
Even in my silent years
When no one seemed to notice me
And no one seemed to care.
But my dreams are not forgotten
There's someone who really cares.
Jesus is bringing my break-through
And I know He's always there.
So, beloved, please remember
To bring your cares to Him.
He'll never leave or forsake you
He's always been your friend.
by Ariel Curtis

Ariel and I had a hallelujah meeting that Sunday at church as we rejoiced and wept together over God's goodness.

The Lord had also been showing me that year (1983)

would be a year of new beginnings – not only for me but for many others in the body of Christ – and Ariel strongly sensed that this was a word for her, too. Later, she had a dream wherein she saw these words in huge block letters suspended above her head almost out of reach – "1983, A YEAR OF NEW BEGINNINGS"! Standing on her toes to pull down the huge letters, she sat on them to claim them for her own! Several months later, the Lord took her out of state to a fresh start and new beginnings. And, through much intercession, my new beginnings, too, were soon to be birthed.

Chapter Six

THE ANOINTING – GOD'S MANTLE FOR MINISTRY

"The Spirit of the Lord God is upon me; because the Lord hath anointed me to preach good tidings unto the meek; He hath sent me to bind up the broken-hearted, to proclaim liberty to the captives, and the opening of the prison to them that are bound."

(Isaiah 61: 1)

It takes the anointing of God to get God's work done. One evangelist says this about the anointing quoting the humorous wisdom of a black minister – "I don't know what it is, but I sure know what it ain't!" Amen! Those who have been ineffective in the work of God's Kingdom know what it's like to become as arrows in the hand of the Almighty when His anointing comes upon them.

Briefly, now, we must go back to that glorious April in 1976 when, through the laying on of hands, I received the manifestation of the baptism in the Holy Spirit. God's power fell in such a way that the ladies gathered in Barbara's living room got so excited they almost forgot I was there! As they took turns hugging me and sharing their own joyful testimonies, I knew I had come to the New Testament fellowship for which I hungered. We came from different denominations - and Pat came out of Mormonism - yet, brought together by the Spirit, we were one - in perfect accord. John 17:21 was quickened to my spirit and I realized, with awe, that Jesus' prayer to the Father that we be one was being fulfilled right before my eyes!

Gabi was ministering elsewhere and the rest of the ladies did not know me. They knew nothing of how powerfully Jesus had been knocking on the door of my heart with His, "I WANT YOU!" nor of how He had led me step by step right up to their door. They did not need to know. They simply believed that when people came it was God who sent them and that they were there to do His bidding. Only later would I fully understand that this was the day the Lord chose to commission me in the presence of witnesses with his holy anointing for ministry.

God uses divine order in His way of doing things and my life was no exception. Through the laying on of hands, His gifts and anointings are imparted (see Acts 13:2,3 and II Timothy 1:6). What happens when God's anointing comes upon us? We are literally "turned into another man" (I Samuel 10:6). Hallelujah! Amen! God equips those He calls. Once His anointing comes upon us, we will never, never again be the same. The anointing is the enabling power that takes us beyond ourselves – thrusting, or projecting, us out into that which God calls us to do. With the anointing then, I was equipped to carry out my first assignment, the writing of a book – something which, in and of myself, I could never do.

The manuscript for *There's More to be Had* was shared first with Pastor Birdsong who agreed that God had truly touched my life. The Lord then instructed that a copy be sent to each of our next of kin along with a note saying it would be published in book form when God opened the door. This was a most difficult step because of what the Lord had already shown me but obedience brought a breakthrough that seemed to, actually, speak the book into existence. (Legs had been put under my faith!) Although it still appeared to be an impossible dream, I now knew that, somehow, the book would be published.

Satan had worked feverishly to prevent the writing and then set upon a plan to wipe out all thought of publication. As I was seeking the Lord for a publisher, Betty strongly encouraged my attendance at a Golgotha ladies' fellowship luncheon "to get needed love and support" during the ongoing fiery trial as well as possible assistance from two ladies concerning book publication. It sounded good and certainly scriptural, but an alarm went up inside. Scriptures came to mind that seemed to refute this warning and, although Eldrin also cautioned against going, I found myself at this meeting wanting to do what was "right." By listening to my head rather than the inner witness, I almost got wiped out.

The great paradox in my life at that time – the joy of God's call on the one hand and the suffering from persecution on the other – gave the deep desire to both rejoice and weep with others in the body of Christ (Romans 12:15). But the discomfiting silence that followed my witness at this gathering let me know I was basically alone with both joy and sorrow. Where was the precious unity of the Spirit that had been so evident in those early meetings before our move?

Following the meeting, I stayed to talk with Astra and Serena. Satan had set me up and now I was about to walk into his trap! Both ladies were church leaders – "Spirit-filled," but from early on there was a definite check especially concerning Astra that I did not understand. There were only good reports. Both were, or, were about to become, officers of Ladies' Aglow (Full Gospel) Fellowship. Why, then, was there such discernment and caution? Wanting to think the best of others – especially of those in the church, I learned it is imperative to listen to the Spirit of God.

After a time with these ladies that was basically fruitless,

I arose to leave only to find myself face to face with Astra attempting, once again, to share the power of God. As I did, all the chill of the Arctic seemed to fill the room. Taken aback by Astra's icy stare, I queried, "You do believe in the baptism in the Holy Spirit, don't you?" (This was not my first time to be on the receiving end of this chilling gaze.) With punctuated precision, her answer came as cold as her stare. "No, I do not," she replied, "You're trying to put God in a neat little box and you just can't do it"!

As I stood there alone (yet not alone!) to face what seemed like all the powers of hell, Serena's silence on the subject thundered in my ears. This was a direct confrontation, but not with the "flesh and blood" (Ephesians 6:12) with which I shared the room! What had been discerned all along now culminated in a deadly blow calculated to put an end to both witness and book publication. It was a strike against the anointing and against the very heart of the message God had called me to write. (The Lord had tried to warn me!) Only by God's grace did I get gracefully out of that place that day. Only by God's grace could I change the subject (off God's power!) telling Astra and Serena I loved them and would see them at church Sunday. Neither responded.

For months, I battled to come out from under an attack that was meant to kill. The worst part was that the devil tried to convince me I was harboring un-forgiveness. With anguish of soul and spirit I cried out to the Lord day and night letting Him know I was willing to do anything – even to the point of going to Astra begging forgiveness on my knees if that was what He would have me do. Only through Ginny, later, did I get release and full assurance that I was not to go to Astra and that there was nothing to ask forgiveness for!

After this incident, the Lord recalled something Pat had

shared at that first meeting at Ft. Wood. Her mother, ill and on her deathbed, I believe, was visited by a beautiful angel who beckoned her to come. The desire to follow was almost overpowering, but Pat's mother, sensing something awry, resisted (the death angel) with all her might and lived to tell the story. The background for this scenario was the Aurora Borealis – the northern lights! More confirmation has since come through others who have discerned this same terrible iciness when confronting Satan's power. We are told in II Corinthians 11:14 not to marvel "for Satan himself is transformed into an angel of light."

With the enemy right in the camp and persecution on all sides, the battle grew even more intense but the Lord had called me to be an overcomer and to press on by faith. Manuscripts were sent out. Only a few had gone out when a door opened for publication through a personal division of a well-known Christian company. We felt this was the door to go through, but knew nothing of the astronomical cost of printing or advertising a book! The Lord took us one step at a time. First, the president of the company (who did not identify himself on the phone but whose voice I recognized from Christian TV) miscalculated the cost. When he called later with a price quote twice as high, we were somewhat "eased in" because of the first quote. We knew we must obey God regardless of cost, and money borrowed to build our house was used for publication. Later this company went out of business because (I believe) of the un-godly tactics used to "fleece the flock."

Satan does not give up easily. There were roadblocks around every corner. (When we know God has called us to do something that will effect all eternity for His kingdom, then we can fairly well know the blocks are Satan's and not God closing doors!) One of Satan's biggest block attempts came when the critique editor dubbed the manuscript "difficult to read," leaving him with "bleak and chilly feelings." Although we would be paying for the book, he recommended that it not be published! Later, I realized this made no sense, whatsoever. At the time, however, oppression fell like a paralyzing blanket. (Later, I wondered if this man was even saved.) The Lord used Eldrin and Janet to quickly identify the enemy and plans were made to proceed.

With the book shipment (October 10th, 1980), came more heavy artillery. After all the work, prayer and battles, a dream was at last being realized and I should have been rejoicing, but as I stood in our garage while one small box after another was unloaded, Satan said, "They are going to sit right here and mildew and rot!" Beneath my breath, I said, over and over, "Lord, they're yours, Lord they're yours. If one person gets saved and filled with the Spirit, it will be worth it." Finally, with a book in hand to review, I was not prepared for yet another attack. Without a publisher's mark, the full impact of responsibility for what had been written hit me. I felt so alone. I could sense the Lord saying, "It's just you and I," but I could not grasp that He was more than enough! Coming in from school just then, Janet said, "Mother, if the Lord had wanted a publisher's mark on your book, don't you think He would have put one on?" With that simple statement the cloud lifted. Praise God for "babes"!

To strengthen me in battle shortly after book arrival, the Lord sent Geri from out of state on a divine mission. Geri was visiting her daughter, a member of Golgotha and, before church on that particular Sunday, Iris, a neighbor of Geri's daughter, who was excited about having met Geri, sought me out. Iris sensed that Geri and I had something in common and insisted that I meet Geri. Busily sharing with others, I totally forgot but the Lord did not! After church, Iris came again tugging at my arm and urging, "We've got to hurry, she's leaving!" In the vestibule, Geri and I met and the Lord took over. Afterwards, I could not even remember her face or name. (The Lord would use this later.) Heavily anointed with God's mantle for ministry, Geri spoke out under the unction of the Holy Ghost to confirm my position in the center of God's will and to bring exhortation to stand fast. The meeting lasted only a few minutes yet how lifted, how encouraged I was after that divine appointment! Little did I know that other such appointments were to follow.

As *There's More to be Had* got into the hands of hungry people, God began to confirm His anointing. The first in ministry to give confirmation was Ginny who had been given the special ability to sense God's anointing on a book simply by picking it up. Later, when a letter came from a well-known minister confirming the anointing, I wept with surprise and gratitude. The Lord spoke, "Why are you surprised? My special anointing was on you all the while you wrote."

I knew this was true. The Lord would not even allow assistance with writing. When a well-versed, educated lady from our church moved nearby, I was sure she was sent to help me write, but the Lord showed me I was not to allow anyone to change my mind in what He wanted said! In time, I would fully understand His wisdom in the matter and that His anointing was sufficient. Later, this special anointing lifted and I began to forget much precious detail the Lord had given me! (The devil is ever at work to steal our blessings.) I tremble to think of the outcome had I not obeyed the Lord within His allotted time frame.

There are many beautiful reports, which can only be touched upon here. Many who read the book said they could not put it down. Some said they sat up late at night to read it. Still others said it could have been their story – that it "flowed" and that they read it three or four times! A Catholic friend I had almost lost touch with had been crying out to God, "There's got to be more to life than this!" when she got my book in the mail. (The Lord prompted sending a copy to everyone on our Christmas card list that year). Her husband was an alcoholic and they were separated, their children were grown and she felt there was nothing left to live for. The book's title so gripped her when she opened the package that she knew at once "it was from God." There is no way to express her excitement and gratitude as she called long distance to say she would be praying for me the rest of her life!

Other reports have involved Missouri Synod Lutheran pastors who, evidently shaken to the core with conviction, changed their sermons dramatically after exposure to the book. The son of an evangelist of Lutheran theological background, who discovered a copy at his parent's home, stated emphatically, "This book needs to be in the hands of every pastor in the Missouri Synod Lutheran church!" One Lutheran minister had his congregation read the book together one Sunday in place of a sermon! A Baptist minister, who read the book, knew, decidedly, that his people needed the end-time message and obtained copies for his congregation to read and study together. Evangelical ministries have requested copies to get out to others as the Lord leads. God's truths know no boundaries and cross all denominational lines.

Not all reports have been so positive. Friends have dropped off our list. Others, while maintaining contact, have carefully avoided any acknowledgment of the book. Some, including pastors, who were enlightened by the Spirit to joyfully receive my witness at first, recognized the price to be paid and quickly went back to their places of "safety." From there, they took up the position of "observing" me

(See Matthew 13:20,21, II Peter 2:21,22 and Hebrews 6:1-6). After we are illuminated (and make the choice to go on with God), Hebrews 10:33 says we become a "gazing stock"!

Because of its content, Christian bookstores have simply refused to place *There's More to be Had* on their shelves. One store owner (disclosing that she was a member of my denominational background) became so flustered and angry she could hardly contain herself as she emphasized how she had the Holy Spirit and there was nothing more to be had. We had previously discerned heaviness in the store, but the Lord made it clear that an attempt must be made to get books on the shelf. While Eldrin prayed at the back, I confronted the powers of darkness up front and, in spite of that woman's indignation, the Lord got ten books into her hands. Later, however, people asking for the book were told the store did not have it! Again, it is dangerous business to fight the Holy Spirit. Christian books have become big business, but few carry God's warnings for an end-time generation and few, according to Ginny, carry God's anointing.

The anointing, which places God's stamp of approval and authority upon a life (or ministry, or book!), also causes controlling devils, operating through religious people, to rise full strength to "keep us in line." The anointing will destroy the yoke of bondage (Isaiah 10:27) for those who want to be free while provoking anger and even rage in those who do not. The anointing will draw or it will repel. There have been times, after witnessing under the anointing, when people (some very close to me) rose right up in my face to attack. The Lord disclosed that controlling devils, who recognized and hated the anointing, were the instigators of these attacks.

In Acts chapter seven we see how controlling devils

instigated the stoning of Stephen. Stephen, who was used of God to warn a "stiff-necked" generation of their resistance to the Holy Ghost, was so anointed that his face was as "the face of an angel" (Acts 6:15). After a lengthy discourse that blasts their theology and "cuts them to the heart," the religious crowd "gnashes on him with their teeth" and stones him to death. Stephen became one of those who "overcame him (Satan) by the blood of the Lamb and by the word of their testimony" who "loved not their lives unto the death" (Revelation 12:11). He saw Jesus seated at the right hand of the Father and the heavens opened for him as he was dying (Acts 7:55,56).

Isaiah 61:1 (heading this chapter) gives God's purpose for the anointing. In Luke 4:18, we find Jesus (who has just returned in the power of the Spirit from His overcoming wilderness experience), reading this Scripture with bold authority in the synagogue in His hometown. He then declares, "This day is this Scripture fulfilled in your ears" (v.21)! Amazed by his anointed words, the people ask, "Is not this Joseph's son?" (v 22). Then, as he goes on to expound, calling himself a prophet, they become so enraged they plan to kill him by casting him headlong over a cliff (v. 23-29)!

What caused the dramatic "about-face" of these people? Held at first by Jesus' anointed Words, they soon reason, "He's one of us – He can't be what He is implying!" (My paraphrase). Religious devils, well aware of the anointing, were busily planting seeds. Murderous thoughts of thwarting God's plan follow. But it was not Jesus' time to be offered up. They could not kill Him nor control Him. He was not under their power. Luke 4:30 says, "But he passing through the midst of them went His way." Anointed to fulfill God's plan, no devil in hell could stop Him.

In Matthew 28:19,20 and Mark 16:15-18, we are given

the directive to go in Jesus' Name. With the added directive in this final hour to wind up the great commission, let us take another look at the following Scripture and God's purpose for the anointing:

> *"The Spirit of the Lord God is upon me; because the Lord hath anointed me to preach good tidings unto the meek; He hath sent me to bind up the brokenhearted, to proclaim liberty to the captives, and the opening of the prison to them that are bound;" (Isaiah 61:1).*

This Scripture (powerfully quickened to my spirit by revelation after the baptism) gives clear understanding of why Satan hates the anointing!

Chapter Seven

PRECEPT UPON PRECEPT, LINE UPON LINE

"For precept must be upon precept, precept upon precept; line upon line, line upon line; here a little, and there a little."

(Isaiah 28:10)

Amazingly, although I identify intensely with God's prophets of old with their prophetic words burning "like a fire in my bones" (Jeremiah 20:9), the position for which I am being proven and groomed is for a time veiled. The Lord does not say right off, "I'm placing you in the prophet's office and, as you know from the Scriptures, the prophets get stoned." No! God in his wisdom knows exactly how much we can handle and when, by His grace, we can handle it. With little or no knowledge of the five-fold ministry, all that transpires in my life in these "latter" days is a new thing unfolding before me (Isaiah 43:19).

The Lord has given me a servant's heart and a ministry of exhortation and encouragement but where, I wonder, do I fit at Golgotha? No longer am I led to teach children and, although we have served on the evangelism team, I know I do not fit into a structured soul-winning program. There have been other areas of service, like designing banners for the new sanctuary and serving on the prayer chain, but top priority is writing a book. Once this foundation is laid, the Lord leaves no stone unturned in letting me know where I fit into the body of Christ.

One Sunday, in the summer of 1981, one of the elders,

in charge of the service, gives a message on talents after which we are told to stand for prayer seeking God diligently about our place in the body of Christ. "Lord," I cry, "where do you want me? I don't seem to fit anywhere any more; my book is not really accepted here and I know I'm not really accepted either." Indeed, my husband, (with righteous indignation carefully hidden), finally presents each elder with a copy of *There's More to be Had* because he feels it their duty to read the book to see where I'm coming from – "whether from God or another source." Of the five elders, only one returns later to comment. Two of their wives, however, read the book and report exuberantly.

Although we do not always understand everything, we hold our leadership in highest esteem as chosen of God. All (it is reported) have been baptized in the Spirit. But, again, from early on, there is growing discernment. In my spirit, I sense discord among the ranks having to do with the power of God. This is eventually confirmed during a talk with pastor Birdsong and, reportedly, resolved. How I pray for Golgotha! Lutheran charismatic ministries, through supportive letters and literature, constantly exhort us to go on with God. God has called us out and He is commanding us, as a church, to move on with him. But something illusive holds us back. The spirit of God is being quenched.

As I stand there that Sunday seeking God with all my heart, a sister in the row ahead turns to say, "You are a toe." I ask her to repeat but know at once from the witness in my spirit that I've heard from God. The devil zooms in, "A toe?! What's a toe? A toe is nothing!" Only the Lord knows of the battle raging just then. Recognizing the spirit of pride, I vow, "Lord, I don't care what you want me to be even if it is a doorkeeper in the house of the Lord (Psalms 84:10), I will do it." Immediately, the devil leaves.

I know God has called me to be a "watchman unto the

house of the Lord" but my head is slow to grasp full implication. That afternoon, as I pray and reflect upon the word, "toe," given that morning – and upon my word back to the Lord to be a doorkeeper, the Lord reminds me that a doorkeeper and a watchman are the same. In no way, had I correlated the two! He then calls my attention to the fact that a toe is important for balance. Later, I learn that the toe, in addition to bringing balance, is important to the circulation and well being of the entire body!

Several Sundays later (August 2nd), I again meet Geri. As mentioned, I do not recall Geri's face or name after our first meeting and, interestingly (by God's design), up to this point nearly a year later, I still have not met her daughter, Terri. So when they enter during Bible study beaming smiles of recognition, I am in a state of consternation. In the spirit, I know Geri, in the natural I do not, and implore the Lord, "Please, Lord, don't let me be embarrassed." The Lord insists she is the one He brought through Iris, and after Bible study Geri turns (bubbling all over with that infectious Holy Ghost joy) to exclaim, "I had a word from the Lord for you, didn't I?!" "You sure did!", I confirm as we greet each other with a holy hug. She tells me she's reading my book and once again for a few brief moments we rejoice in the precious unity of Spirit we share. Only later will I fully understand this special communion of our spirits.

Prayer meeting (August 11) holds another blessing. In answer to my heart's cry (growing in intensity) for ministers of deliverance, I meet Ginny. Witness comes that Ginny (like Gabi) is surely God's chosen vessel and as she shares concern for her church – how the Spirit of God is often quenched, I sense liberty to share my own burden for Golgotha and to ask for prayer. To my surprise, Ginny already knows of the problem and is praying! How I rejoice that someone sensitive to the Spirit has knowledge of a "delicate" situation I've had to wait very carefully on the Lord to share.

It seems the Lord has given me the special ability to sense, or see, as it were, with the eye of the Spirit into the internal workings of the church. I do not understand this. Neither do I question it, or consider it strange. I simply know it is so. This ability, however, places me in a precarious position. I am keenly aware that my words and actions must be carefully led by the Spirit or they can be used as Satan's tools of entrapment. Only later will I understand that to "see with the eye of the Spirit" is an enabling gift of the watchman's ministry.

The Lord's desire for Golgotha to move on in the Spirit burns within me and I know we must be equipped for battle. So when one of the elders begins a teaching series in the Sunday morning adult Bible study on spiritual warfare, I get really excited. At last, we are on track! Excitement mounts just after this series is completed when Ginny announces plans to visit Cover Church. They believe the Lord is leading them to a deliverance ministry there. Prayer prevails, but Ginny reports later they would have been "thrown out on their ear!" Disappointment is keen. Had they been accepted, Golgotha would have derived direct benefit because of our close ties to Cover Church. (Later, the concept becomes clear. Cover Church serves as our spiritual authority or "covering.")

As the burden for Golgotha grows, I feel led to share with Elder Mistik, upon whom I've surely sensed God's anointing. He is revered as a prophet and certainly seems to fit the role. Yet there is that inner caution that compels me to look to the Lord alone, praying much before a meeting held in our home on October 3rd. "Beneficial" is the word used in a diary entry to describe the meeting lasting from 7:30 to midnight, but I'm sure I know in my spirit even then, that this is only wishful thinking. There has been growing apprehension about the upcoming meeting (deep within, I sense what God has given me will, ultimately, not be received) and I must be certain of the Lord's leading in sharing with Elder Mistik. During prayer the day before, the Lord gives a strong green light through the following word:

> *"My child, I know your thoughts, your feelings (reservations). I am sending you forth as a light in dark places. My sheep hear my voice. You have heard my voice very clearly in the past. Go forward and trust me that you have heard my voice again. The task I set before you is not an easy one, yet I must use those who are available to sound my prophetic warning. The storm clouds gather very quickly and time is short. My people must be equipped for battle; sin must be purged out. Self must die."*

Even before this, the Lord gives some pretty strong clues as to the position and assignment ahead. On a scrap of paper which I had not as yet started dating, this word is hurriedly scribbled as the Lord speaks into my spirit at least a year or so before:

> *"I want you to bring my deliverance to the oppressed. Fear not, I will not let you be ashamed – I will lift you up. I will give you a mouth to speak in boldness. I have called you out. You are my handmaiden. Fear no man."*

Other notes are on this paper. Joshua 1:9 and Jeremiah 1:6-8, 17 – having to do with the call of God and the command to be courageous in the face of man – are jotted down. The Lord speaks, especially, through Jeremiah 1:7 – *"But the Lord said unto me, Say not, I am a child: for thou shalt go to all that I shall send thee, and whatsoever I command thee thou shalt speak."* Written down, also, are these words: "I have made thee a watchman unto the house of the Lord" and "if you do not tell them, this sin will be upon you" (my paraphrase of Ezekiel 3:17,18). Notes on "toe" and "balance" are added before the October meeting.

From these and other notes, I share with Elder Mistik what the Lord has been showing me. Of deep concern are the hungry, hurting sheep often wounded even more deeply by someone in a leadership capacity. Often, the Lord places these bleeding sheep across my path or on my doorstep. Jesus' words from Matthew 18:6,7 have been burning in my heart – *"whoso shall offend one of these little ones which believe in me, it were better for him that a millstone were hanged about his neck and that he were drowned in the depth of the sea...woe to that man by whom the offense cometh!"* I sense Jesus' fiery jealousy over the sheep and His concern for their growth and well-being.

Of equal concern is the acute awareness of the need for deliverance within the body of Christ. Pastor Birdsong's wife, Wren, grows worse while others in a similar state are also hospitalized in the "mental health" center where (I know by the Spirit) demons have a haven. People with deliverance needs are flowing into Golgotha and it is becoming more and more obvious that it is God who is sending them there.

Elder Mistik makes many notes as we talk and we seem to have communion and agreement on all shared. Eldrin expresses concern that we may still be tied to a form of religion (Lutheranism) and, somewhere during the evening, Elder Mistik mentions a vision given one of the elders of black-robed monks groaning and chanting as they encircle the church. We sense the oppressive heaviness of this vision, but not until later in the evening do we recall, with astonishment, that Luther was a monk! It seems quite obvious, from this vision, that a spirit of Lutheranism does have a hold upon us.

The Lord gives one word that cannot be shared. For days (or perhaps weeks) prior to this meeting the Holy Spirit has been crying, "Ai!", in my spirit. This is followed by the words, "There's sin in the camp!" Not only is this word exceedingly heavy with God's holiness, but there is a definite check that it is not to be shared. The account of Ai in Joshua 7 tells how Joshua seeks the face of God when Israel loses the battle at Ai (which should have been easily won) and is shown that the loss is due to an "accursed thing" in the camp. As the Lord pinpoints Israel's sin at Ai, I know He is about to pinpoint the sin at Golgotha. I do not like what He is showing me.

The Lord does not leave off speaking after the meeting with Elder Mistik. Soon, the word "catalyst" comes, repeatedly, to arrest my full attention. The Spirit of God moves powerfully upon me as I look up the word showing me I will be used as a catalyst at Golgotha. (A catalyst is something used to speed a reaction while itself remaining unchanged!) I know this new word ties in with "toe" and "watchman" and then, when another word, "conduit," comes on the heels of all this, I laugh, "Lord, I've got the message, you don't have to give me any more words! I know what a conduit is – it's something through which something flows." Nevertheless, the Lord directs me to my dictionary and a second very significant meaning – protector!!

The words and their meanings come tickertape fashion each building, beautifully, upon the other. The word, "conduit," gives more understanding of what it means to "see with the eye of the Spirit into the internal workings of the church." If equipped with a sensor, the conduit (in addition to being a channel and a protector) could sense or "feel" that which flows through it. So, by the Spirit of God (my Sensor!), I am given the ability to sense or "feel" that which "flows" through the church. Imagine my excitement, then, when I realize that the watchman and the doorkeeper like the conduit, are protectors! Although at this point I still see, to some degree, as through a glass darkly (I Corinthians 13:12), the Lord lets me know He is laying it all out for me "precept upon precept, line upon line – here a little and there a little" (Isaiah 28:10)!

Despite telling the Lord His message is clear, still another word follows shortly. Literally lifting off the page of *Come Away My Beloved*, comes this question – "Will ye resist if I choose to make you My *aqueduct* (my emphasis)?" It pricks my heart to the core and deepens even further the conviction to obey the Lord regardless of cost. The Lord intends to use me. Of this, He leaves no room for doubt. I will simply be a channel for His Spirit at Golgotha.

At prayer meeting (November 3), I share what the Lord is unfolding and Ginny responds. Just the day before "a person of significance" (from Golgotha) visits them – "soaking up all they share (about deliverance) during an hour and a half" – concluding, "We must get Pastor and Wren here!" Ginny and I try to wait carefully on the Lord and names are not mentioned but I believe this person (told by the Wrenchers to keep in close contact with me "Because the Lord is using me at Golgotha") is Elder Mistik. Ginny then says, "The Lord is trying to place His mantle of deliverance over Golgotha Lutheran church and without intercession, nothing will happen." No wonder people are flowing into Golgotha! No wonder the burden to pray! The Lord tried to put this mantle on her church, Ginny says, but "for some reason" He lifted it back off. To me, the reason seems obvious – her church would not accept it.

Then, with eyes riveted upon me, Ginny expounds (in essence), "I see a wheel – there are spokes in the wheel, a hub in the center. You are right in the center of that hub. The spokes are people at Golgotha. Soon they are going to start speaking out (against you)! Be very careful how you listen and even more careful what you say." Sensing something terribly insidious just ahead (a device for entrapment!), I instantly commit to the Lord, fervently praying, "Lord, set a guard over my mouth!"

That Sunday, I am again compelled to talk to Elder Mistik. He says I am the third person to confront him about the heaviness in the service that morning – one person described it as a "wet blanket" settling down. We talk of the lack of freedom in praise and worship, but then, strangely enough, as we continue to talk, Elder Mistik, seems to actually disagree with much of what he agreed to in the meeting the month before! Although three people have just confirmed it, he questions that there is bondage in the church. He says there may be a "fear of Lutheranism" rather than actual bondage to it. This is perplexing and discouraging especially in light of the somber vision of the black-robed monks he had shared.

Elder Mistik goes on. He says this fear may be on me. I agree to fear – but to fear of speaking out and of being rejected. He prays (binding fear) and then, as I share more words recently received (except for the word, Ai, and Ginny's vision of the wheel which can not be shared), he says I seem to have "an almost prophetic role." He says the Lord has given me "much" and that he thinks the day will come when the door will open for my testimony. Ironically, he also prophesies, unknowingly. "The day will come," he says, "when you will have to speak out leaving what you have said at the altar – criticism and rejection can be expected." He says he has been going over notes and will need to meet with us again soon. That meeting, however, will never occur.

At some point, I fully comprehend that God is placing me in the prophet's office and, here or there as God opens doors, I begin to (innocently!) share. Now, this is not pretension on my part. To acknowledge God's gifts and calling is not a show of pride (I Samuel 9:19). To be called by Almighty God for any purpose leaves me awestruck and to serve Him is my greatest joy. I am ready to be used in any capacity, which has been proven to the Lord by my willingness to accept, without question, the position of a toe. In God's timing, I simply speak forth that which He is disclosing and giving full liberty and unction to share. Later, I might be tempted to retract it all.

Chapter Eight

THE SIN IN THE CAMP IS PIN-POINTED

"There is an accursed thing in the midst of thee, O Israel:
thou canst not stand before thine enemies, until ye take
away the accursed thing from among you."

(Joshua 7:13)

Praise the Lord for his gracious word to forewarn and protect! Soon after the word comes through Ginny, Satan rises up in a particularly diabolical way. With big guns poised and aimed at the center of the "wheel," he uses the "spokes" as ammunition!

Within a two week period, four people (of considerable clout) become Satan's emissaries. Two (with knowledge of a certain situation) bring a "word of direction" (rebuke!) to whip me in line. One actually motions as we stand in church for prayer pulling my head down in humiliating fashion to whisper in my ear! Instantly warned by the Spirit, my only action (with pounding heart) is to nod and return to my seat. (Praise God for His direction in advance!) A third sister is used to bring chagrin. (All, incidentally, are friends of a "spoke" previously used.) The fourth is an elder who, after Eldrin expresses grievance over the lack of joy and freedom in the church, sets Eldrin down, lays hands on him and prays that he will, in effect, accept the "status-quo"! Caught off-guard (submitting to this man in authority), Eldrin struggles for days to come out from under the heaviness (death!) this "prayer" ministers to his spirit. (Eldrin and I are one and what affects one affects both!)

Striking at a vulnerable area, it is Satan's intent to break through our line of defense. And, indeed (even with previous direction), we might well have been swept off course had it not been for the Lord's special word through Ginny. By God's grace, we stand fast with a guard over our mouth while Satan's attempt to stain our credibility (by getting us to react in the flesh) fizzles out.

The remainder of 1981 proves equally interesting as the warfare, persecution and confirmation continue. Once more, as I stand in the prayer line (November 19) the last night of a special crusade meeting at a local hotel, the Lord deems fit to confirm His anointing. The crusade speaker, Maynard Waters, singles me out. "My sister," he says, "you do not need prayer – the anointing of God is all over you!" He then directs me to minister to ladies standing by! Only the Lord knows how precious such confirmation is, as we maintain our front line stand against all the wiles and accusations of the enemy!

That Sunday (November 22), brother Onn from Cover Church (who had the word about my son two years before) is back at Golgotha. During an anointed teaching, he challenges the adult Bible study with this question, "Are you willing to raise the dead should the Lord call you to do so?"! Then, emphasizing the Lord's desire to use each person in the body of Christ, he goes on, "The Lord is not interested in raising up a HIERARCHY in the church" (my emphasis). The statement could have been shot from a gun! Instantly, powerfully, the Lord confirms a word He has been speaking into my spirit for days – "The devil is trying to raise up a hierarchy at Golgotha." Again, I can only think, "My God, what do you want me to do with this (revelation)?!" His instruction is precise, "Pray much and wait carefully on Me."

Another mighty confirmation comes less than two weeks later, but in between is a letter to our Elder Nutral. Immediate opposition rises with the spiritual warfare teaching at Golgotha and, among other "happenings," one of the elder's wives is hit with cancer. The entire church is asked to pray for Carrie reporting back to our elders what we may have gotten from the Lord. After two hours of prayer (November 25), the following letter is comprised:

"Dear Elder Nutral,

As I drew aside this afternoon to intercede for Carrie, I asked the Lord to remove my own thoughts and to reveal those things He would want me to see. Although I was interceding in the Spirit for Carrie, thoughts about Golgotha kept coming to me.

The Lord gave me a vision for Golgotha at it's inception – not a 'picture' vision, if you will, but a vision in my mind's eye of a church filled with the fullness of God's power – a true New Testament church – where the glory of God comes down, where the fruits of the Spirit are flowing and the gifts of the Spirit are in full operation. At that time, He also gave me a burden for Golgotha – especially for its leadership and began to show me things I needed to be praying for. I realized I was to be an intercessor, but did not fully understand the significance of this until recent months.

I had been praying for a long time in the area of deliverance and for the baptismal fire and power at Golgotha but, during the summer, my prayers in these areas really intensified. Shortly afterwards, Elder (blank) began to teach on spiritual warfare! During this time the Lord showed me something else (which I do not feel led to share at this time) having to do with His desire for deliverance.

The attacks of the enemy have intensified, bringing us up to the present. During my encounter with Jesus as the baptizer, He clearly showed me that the devil would try to snuff out every work that God was raising up in power. Although this was a new revelation for me, it is not new. The pattern is clearly seen all through the Bible.

God is allowing us to see the enemy in his fury. What is happening to Carrie concerns the whole body at

Golgotha. God is challenging us to go forward in faith, to
believe His word and stand fast regardless of the wiles of
the enemy. We've only just begun!

In Jesus' love,
Chris Linneman

The warfare that surrounds writing this letter (and
getting it into the mail as directed by the Lord before losing
courage) is unbelievable. Does it mean the Lord plans to
use the letter to bring about a change at Golgotha? Or, again,
is this only wishful thinking?

Contact with Elder Nutral has been rather shallow. I
recall one brief encounter the previous year – an inquiry
concerning Hydie who, also assigned to Elder Nutral, is
hospitalized. I learn she has been admitted to the mental
health center.

Immediate heaviness, unrest, the sure inner knowing
that something is askew, had accompanied meeting Hydie.
Our husbands (with common bond) set a date to get together,
but before they arrive the discernment is so strong I'm beside
myself. (Whatever is on Hydie is trying to come on me!) As
I try to pray for Hydie, I literally plead, "Lord, is this (evil)
on me (something I need to confess and get rid of) or is it
on her? I've got to know!" The Lord does not leave me
hanging. Before the evening ends, three devils (lurking in
her background) are uncovered – alcoholism, Mormonism
and suicide (her young brother was a victim of suicide)!

As yet, I've not met Ginny, but I realize the gravity of a
situation where Hydie not only harbors but also nurtures
her devils. Yet, admired as a "gutsy lady," she ministers –
I'm on the receiving end of a "word" or two. (The Lord
later reveals that such people are a "house divided against
itself.") I learn that Hydie's hospitalization is the result of
attempted suicide and finally tell her straight out that the
devil is trying to take her life. But she wants no part of this

kind of talk – at least not from me. Sadly, her preschool child follows suit. On prescription drugs and hyper to the hilt, he, too, has spent a year in (the children's psychiatric ward of) the mental health center.

With genuine dismay, I wonder why church leadership who profess to know the power of God – those upon whom Hydie leans (with her husband temporarily away) – would place one desperately needing deliverance in a world system that knows nothing of her real need? But, then, Wren Birdsong was ushered down the same path and later others will follow. Each, in their turn, will leave Golgotha as bound as they came...

The inquiry concerning Hydie had brought a definite check. Elder Nutral seems to have little awareness of the spiritual realm and, along the way, there has been no leading to share. He is, however, a likeable, mild-mannered man upon whom I sense no actual heaviness – the devil seems uninterested in using him. Why, then, the warfare surrounding my letter? Undoubtedly, wicked entities in high places are threatened by its contents sure to be shared among the ranks. In any event, I do not hear from Elder Nutral. In addition, the elder admonished by the Wrenchers to keep in touch remains anonymous.

Golgotha's "something illusive" is next confirmed December 5th as I share with Warren Black, the Men's Full Gospel speaker, a certain tape I had listened to that afternoon. Out of the blue, he asks if I am aware that this brother (on the tape) has been involved in "shepherdship"? Again, the word, shepherdship, like hierarchy, quickens like a gunshot! The power of God absolutely envelops me. Brother Black doesn't know it, but the very fact that this subject (of which I know nothing) is brought up is God! "No!", I reply, in a state of shock as he adds just one more thing to the subject. "Yes," he says, "the sheep have a tendency to swallow everything the leadership feeds them."

Red flags are flying!! If I've ever heard the word, shepherdship, it has had no negative connotation, but now the Holy Spirit shows me that this shepherdship (like hierarchy) means lordship not of God and that it has definitely permeated Golgotha. I sense God's holy indignation and revelation so powerful I must lower my head to keep from falling out under that power. Brother Black asks what's wrong and I explain, "The Lord has just confirmed that this is in my church!" In response to my concern, he gives assurance that "praying much and waiting carefully on the Lord" is exactly the right thing to do.

The "sin in the camp" has certainly been pinpointed! The Lord has been giving discernment all along in a delicate area, indeed, – one in which I have not cared to look. Now it is even clearer why the Lord would not allow the word, "Ai", to be shared with Elder Mistik. Some innocent sheep might have become the scapegoat! In the "yoke" with Jesus, I cannot bear the thought.

Interestingly enough, really heavy messages on "submission" and "relationships" come down that Sunday (December 6) through both Pastor Birdsong (in charge of adult Bible study) and Elder Mistik (who delivers the sermon that morning.) Time must be taken (doing battle!) to come out from under the oppressive heaviness of these messages. That afternoon a member calls wanting to know "What's going on with the leadership?"! Eldrin keeps the conversation light. In spite of what we know – in spite of what the Lord is showing us, the Holy Spirit guards our conversation. We are not to speak against the leadership.

Often, matter-of-factly, Eldrin says to me, "Chris, the Lord has given you so much more (revelation) than Pastor Birdsong." Quick with reproof, I cannot deny the fact that, long before, this portion of Scripture was quickened to my spirit:

> *"O how I love thy law! It is my meditation all the day.*
> *Thou through thy commandments hast made me wiser than*
> *mine enemies: for they are ever with me. I have more*
> *understanding than all my teachers: for thy testimonies*
> *are my meditation. I understand more than the ancients,*
> *because I keep thy precepts."*
>
> *(Psalm 119:97-100)*

Neither can I deny the fact that the Lord, from early on, has given me this reminder – *"For unto whomsoever much is given, of him shall be much required"* (Luke 12:48).

Up in arms over the revelation and confirmation exposing him, Satan comes in like a flood. Dangling his bait before me day and night, he tempts, "The Lord has shown you much but you are unrecognized. Why don't you stand up and tell them (the leadership) who you are and what you have received from God?"!

At the onset, God gives this word: *"Humble yourselves therefore under the mighty hand of God, that He may exalt you in due time"* (I Peter 5:6). I have no intention of following Satan's suggestion – no matter how attractive – and God's word is a rock beneath – yet the power of this thing becomes such that, eventually, in spite of constant resistance, I become caught in a dreadful hammerlock.

By prayer meeting that Tuesday (December 8), the "burden" for Golgotha is so heavy I cannot pray. I tell the others to pray, but I can't wait to get out and get home. Once home, I slump in a chair with lethargy so unbearable I can only cry from my heart for help. Janet comes bounding down the stairs all excited over Christmas, her favorite time of year. But I cannot bear the thought. I must have sat there for an hour when the phone rings. It's Ginny! "Chris," she says, "I don't know what's wrong, but I have such a burden for you." Praise God, He's heard my cry! And praise God for body ministry through vessels sensitive to His Spirit and available for His use!

Knowing my readiness to serve the Lord, the devil is able, ever so subtly, to turn the burden (for Golgotha's deliverance) into a false burden. I didn't know there was such a thing (A burden from the Lord will not be unbearable)! The latest revelation concerning Golgotha (like the word, Ai,) can not be shared with even Ginny and, seemingly alone with the "whole ball of wax," I take on, unknowingly, what is Jesus' load to carry. I need to go before God's throne Ginny says, asking forgiveness for opening the door to Satan in the first place (by taking on a load that is not mine to carry). Then, I need to do battle with Satan. My hand will scarcely function to write Ginny's instructions but, once again, with his schemes uncovered, Satan must go. Through the Word, the Name and the blood of Jesus, the awful lethargic oppression lifts and the true burden of the Lord for Golgotha returns.

Starting with the revelation beginning in the summer, the battle's duration is six months. Throughout, I am acutely aware of Satan's plan to push me out ahead of God's timing. (The uprising through the "spokes" is but one last mighty thrust.) Once again, had he succeeded, God's plan to use me at Golgotha would have been aborted. Through disobedience, I would have come out from under the Lord's protective covering and the results for me could have been devastating.

With Golgotha's sin uncovered, I realize it should have come as no surprise. For at least a year before the meeting with elder Mistik, I have known the day would come when the Lord will send me before church leadership with a word. In a continual vision, I actually see and hear myself expounding before them. But there is a bothersome aspect to all this. The Lord has shown me that neither I nor the Word will be received. Why, I wonder, would it be necessary to give a word if only to be rejected?! The scriptural answer has already come but, again, for my own protection, full implication is veiled. For that which is to come, the Lord knows He must buffer me about with even more confirmation – profound confirmation that will have to come through His anointed servants.

Chapter Nine

SATAN'S WRATH AGAINST DELIVERANCE

"The devil is come down unto you, having great wrath, because he knoweth that he hath but a short time."
(Revelation 12:12)

A new year, 1982, arrives and with it comes continued hope and prayer for a breakthrough at Golgotha in spite of all the Lord has been disclosing. But January 3rd, the first Sunday of the New Year and Millie's farewell Sunday, is not a good harbinger. Millie really loves the Lord and is looking forward to serving Him in a new location and capacity. But, alas! The morning brings no mention of her departure, no prayers or blessings by leadership with the laying on of hands at the front of the church – none of the usual procedure for those leaving the area. There is no doubt that Millie's decision has had leadership approval and, from all appearance, she has enjoyed good standing in the church. Why then this "oversight"?

While awaiting an announcement – thinking surely I remember correctly that it is Millie's last Sunday, the Lord gives clear discernment. I have not seen Millie – perhaps she is not here – but, sensing her anguish in my spirit, I hurry to find her after the service. Millie stands alone oblivious to those around her. Shocked bewilderment covers her face. *Yes*, it is her last Sunday and *why was there no acknowledgment?* "Do not receive it, Millie!", I admonish strongly. "It's simply the devil's attack against you because you've been involved in something called deliverance."

Millie is confused and hurting, but I know she understands what I'm talking about.

Millie and I had been drawn together by the Lord. Her vision of an hourglass with the last grains of sand running out was especially thrilling to me for the same vision burns in my heart. (Dreams of a church banner must be shelved as other matters take precedence.) Millie's had other visions, too, – beautiful visions of the Lord's desire to use Golgotha. In addition, we have something else in common. Millie, too, had been led to the Wrenchers.

Excited over the ministry of the Wrencher's, Millie and a friend had tried to share their enthusiasm with leadership. Perhaps this was the reason Golgotha's "person of significance" paid the Wrenchers a visit. But despite the then obvious enthusiasm of this leader, contact with the Wrenchers was frowned upon and then forbidden.

With this background – plus knowing the morning's attack is aimed squarely at me specifically at this time, I'm not to be intimidated. This is the morning I have purposed in my heart to see Pastor Birdsong. In my purse is a large article from a local newspaper. Complete with family picture, it glorifies God by beautifully highlighting the fruit of the Wrencher's Christian walk in their field of secular employment. It will serve as an opener with which to approach Pastor Birdsong. I will be asking permission to get ministry from the Wrenchers.

What if my request is refused? In my heart, I already know the answer. The Lord has set before me an open door I must go through. Still, my concern was shared with Geri who had visited Golgotha during Christmas the week before. With her hands clasped firmly over mine and looking up to heaven with the steel-like determination of one who has decided to follow Jesus all the way, Geri had simply said, "Christal, *Jesus is your Lord*." Oh, how well I knew this truth! Yet the Spirit's confirmation through Geri brought strength, comfort. While trying in every way possible to submit to authority, I knew that, ultimately, my obedience must be to the Lord. Nothing of what the Lord had been revealing was shared with Geri but, at that time, she too, confirmed Golgotha's bondage attributing it to leadership.

Pastor Birdsong glances at the article. He knows of the Wrenchers, he says (which, of course, is no surprise), admitting Millie was helped. He feels their ministry is "legitimate" and that they are "seeking to follow the Lord" – however, they are "not under church authority" and "God's Word tells us to obey those over us." He wishes "there were some way to get them into Golgotha – but, if they won't come"...his voice trails off. The Wrenchers attend Clone church having placed themselves under its authority from the beginning. But "for some reason" the Lord won't let them join. I say nothing to Ginny, but the Lord shows me their ministry would have been severely quenched or even killed had they joined the church.

Because I am "mature in the Lord," my permission is granted. It is troublesome that others might be denied, but for now I must be content that my own way is clear. Leaning heavily on the Lord in Pastor Birdsong's office, I realize only later that the Lord – knowing I must remain in good standing in the church – has the whole thing in hand. My time to "rebel" has not yet come.

The step taken this morning seems to set off an avalanche in the spiritual realm. Anyone touching deliverance is targeted. My notes begin to read like something from *This Present Darkness*, Frank Perreti's best-seller of later years. Ginny comes under the attack covered earlier. Judd and Dede, a young Golgotha couple who are "instant in season and out of season" with ministry, are pummeled unmercifully. Telephone conversations concerning the subject of deliverance are often interrupted by loud static noise and sometimes even cut off. Severe headaches, nausea and vomiting are not unusual following these conversations.

Suddenly, those given to seizures become as puppets in the hands of an unseen puppeteer. While one stays home battling unusually severe attacks, another is literally thrown in the church isle one Sunday. With righteous indignation – even as the elders attempt hushed ministry over the victim in the aisle, I fervently pray, "Lord, get Judd out there!" The Lord honors that prayer but soon Judd is called on the carpet. Judd is bold – he prays with faith and power but, reportedly, "people don't like the way he prays."

Before meeting with the Wrenchers, awareness of my own position in the path of the avalanche heightens. Not ignorant of Satan's devices, I ask Ginny to keep me in prayer. I'm also impressed to anoint all doors and windows with oil pleading the blood of Jesus over them. Then, almost predictably, the day before my first appointment, something occurs to leave me with an even deeper appreciation of the precious blood covering of Jesus Christ.

March 29th is a beautiful day. Our cat, Tuffy, runs to greet me as I return to the house from outside. As I lean over to put Tuffy down in the kitchen, I am met, with amazement, by the plaid in the kitchen carpet as it lifts, swims and runs together weirdly about my feet. Abruptly, I straighten only to discover that my eyes are crossed. Everything is in doubles or triples! Corneal abnormality had been diagnosed years before, but I know this is not the problem. Sensing, immediately, the evil presence behind this unholy attack, I begin to confess, over and over, "I'm under the blood of Jesus!"

"You are going blind!" Comes the voice of the enemy. Then, "Even if you have surgery, they will not be able to help you" and, finally, "You will not be able to see to get to the Wrenchers tomorrow." The third threat is the clincher! Satan's fiendish attempt to frighten me from the Wrenchers has caused him to overplay his hand. Later, I recall how the attack had tried to come on, fleetingly, almost unnoticed, the week before and realize hell's agents must have gotten their wires crossed in timing!

As absurd as it may seem, this potentially terrifying experience becomes one of total peace and victorious joy from beginning to end. I am going forward to "possess the land" as the Lord is commanding and I know I'm in the center of His perfect will. My faith is instantly activated. I can sense His protective hand upon me. A bubble-like shield completely surrounds me! It's as large as my hands stretched out to either side and could not be more tangible should I be able to see or feel it with my physical senses. I'm aware of something else very tangible. Just outside the perimeter of this invincible shield, fear literally bounces up and down in feverish, but wholly futile attempts to get in!

The Lord speaks, "This (that you are now going through) is for (on behalf of) the body of Christ!" His wonderful presence and protection are glorious – *absolutely glorious* and, right there, I say, "Lord, please don't let me forget this experience!" I'm caught up in praise and worship, but know the importance of waiting carefully on the Lord. As I make my way to the phone, my heart begins to palpitate wildly and I can feel sickness entering right down to the marrow of my bones.

It is shortly before 10:30 a.m. – *God's timing*. Ginny is just home from her all-night job. On separate phones, she and Carl seek the Lord carefully for some time before Ginny exclaims, "There it is, there it is, I see it!" Through the discerning of spirits (I Corinthians 12:10), Satan is pinpointed! Not until the next day, however, does Ginny explain. A cobra, fastened to the back of my eyes, is looking through. Sickly whitish hues filter through its own (vertical) eyes. Ginny commands Satan to go in Jesus' Name, tells him he will not see through eyes God has given me. As she ministers, I fully expect my vision to clear at any second, but it does not. The victorious spirit, however, remains. I'm under the blood of Jesus and Satan is a defeated foe! This "thing" has to lift and when is not important. "Just listen carefully to the Lord when you get off the phone," Ginny instructs, "and call us if you need us."

"Fill the house with praise music," is the Lord's next command. From records already stacked, the first song to play is "We are the soldiers of the Army of Salvation" – *the only spiritual warfare song in our entire collection of praise music*! Again, God's sovereign hand! Words never really heard before, go straight into my spirit – "though the foes of hell and darkness come head-on against us, by suffering temptation we are tried, and we know there's not a power that can overtake us with the love of Jesus on our side." AMEN!! Faith and power rise up mightily within me. It is finished! Victory is mine!

By now, my balance, too, is completely off, but I dance and shout the victory all over the living room. Doubt was not to enter so I had been unable to look at my eyes but now I march upstairs to the big bath mirror. I have to get real close to even see my eyes but see that they are *perfectly straight*. "I knew it, I knew it," I shout, "devil, you are a lying spirit!" (Ginny confirms next day that it was indeed, a lying spirit.)

The Lord's command for what turns out to be the remainder of the day is simply, "Rest in my presence." No work is to be done. I am very weak. Much of the day is spent outdoors basking in the Lord's precious presence and protection. Little by little, hell's assignment lifts and by the time Eldrin returns home from out of town, all is near normal. Something notable then takes place. My husband does not understand. Upset, he begins to reprimand. Strife tries to enter and the assignment begins to return! I have to leave quickly in order to get back under the Lord's protective covering. Some who read this will not understand, but I knew the importance of obeying, explicitly, each of the Lord's commands. Shortly afterwards, I am given the all clear signal.

Some may wonder why it was necessary to spend the better part of the day "incapacitated" or why I did not just "rebuke Satan and get him off" in the first place. I can only say the battle was not mine but the Lord's. All was filtered through His protective hand. The only "sword" to be used in this particular situation was the blood of Jesus. The garment of praise was my mantle, the joy of the Lord my strength and the peace of the Holy Ghost my inner umpire. It was a time of complete obedience, complete trust in the Lord. And, the Lord's word at the onset was of utmost significance. It was a time of passing through on behalf of the body of Christ which, at the time, I could not fully comprehend. I did know even then, however, that my position was that of a forerunner. Later, of course, I would fully understand that those called to lead must be willing to go ahead of, or pave the way, for the body of Christ. The experience was a dramatic demonstration of the complete protection of the blood of Jesus Christ. It was also a dramatic demonstration of Satan's vehement hatred of deliverance and his attempt to block it from the body of Christ.

This attack was no real surprise. Soon after the baptism in the Spirit, I was given a very significant dream to prepare me for the confrontations ahead. In the dream, I am in a lovely park area waiting to minister to a deeply oppressed young woman who disappears suddenly in search of her small child. Sensing her grave danger and knowing by the Spirit where she has gone, I follow, quickly, to a stairway leading to an underground pavilion. As I begin to descend the stairs, I am confronted by a horribly ominous presence just before a huge hand reaches down from the shadowy stairwell for my throat. I stand between Satan and his captive and he is after my life! But, now, with the precious name of Jesus ever on my lips, I awaken in great victory rebuking Satan in that all-powerful Name. This dream, like the latest skirmish, openly exposed Satan's wrath against both deliverance and those God raises up to be His deliverers.

The next day Carl meets me at the door with a wrench "to pry off demons" and Ginny says it is probably time (after yesterday) to get out of the ministry! The Wrenchers have a sense of humor, but they are not frivolous in what God has called them to do. Nor are they novices. With a "root" deliverance ministry, they work from two sheets of criteria the Lord has given them. False Worship and Idolatry heads one sheet and Sexual Impurity (to which rejection opens the door) heads the other. Every Christian, they say, needs deliverance from both. At this point, some may be confused and others indignant, but these are the days when "the axe is (being) laid unto the root" (Matthew 3:10). We must will to be free from all that hinders serving God. Because of abuse – plus the teaching that Christians don't need deliverance, this needed ministry has been all but thrown out. We must have the balance that only the Holy Spirit can bring. It must be remembered, too, that deliverance is not an end in itself. The "house" that is swept clean must be filled with the Spirit (See Jesus' warning in Matthew 12:43-45).

Four sessions with the Wrenchers include times of sharing. There are manifestations – enough to know something is definitely taking place – and I praise God for competent ministers. Rest is the order of the day following ministry not only because it is needed, but to allow the Holy Spirit to continue His work. Forgiveness is an important part of ministry and time is spent between sessions allowing the Holy Spirit to bring back incidents from the past and people who need to be forgiven. A cleansing, healing process takes place as I weep before the Lord during (what I recall as) a two-hour sitting.

During the second session (especially significant), Ginny has two visions. We stand before God's throne in one as the Father talks with Ginny and Carl – tells them they have done well and that their ministry is pleasing to Him. After some time, the Father, placing His left hand on the throne, reaches out with His right hand and touches the left side of my head. "See," He says, "I am reaching out and removing scars...from the dark corridors of time." Ginny sees the Father's hand sweeping away cobwebs from a long dark corridor. (She tells me freedom from mind binders of the past can be expected.) Finally, Carl hands me over to the Father who takes me in His arms and with His entire attention on me glances at times at Carl and nods. There is a word for me: "Fear not, My child, you are in the palm of My hand. I am pleased with you. I have brought you into a level with the Father you have not known – a broader, deeper spiritual realm. I am bringing you into My rest."

In the next vision, Ginny sees a wall three to four feet high on either side of an opening leading into what appears to be a circle (sheepfold). Jesus, Himself, is the opening (door). Three times He repeats (referring to Himself) "This is the doorway" (John 10:1-16). She watches me go up to the doorway and then to actually appear to be inside Jesus – becoming as one with Him. We remain there – in the doorway – for a time. Ginny is able to see inside the enclosure, which has wide horizons, depth – the appearance of haziness suggesting great expansion. Later, Ginny gets this second part to the vision: Jesus takes me in His arms and seems to say, "Here we go!" as we step out together into that great expanse I understand clearly as future ministry. I am reminded of the launching pad and whatever lies beyond!

Geri is back at Golgotha on Easter, April 11th, and in another God-ordained encounter, I share that I am receiving ministry, the attack and battle fatigue. Geri stands with me against Satan's power – says the Lord would never have allowed such an attack had He not known I was ready. (I know this is true.) She, too, has a word that I am entering God's rest and, as she prays for me, the words, "revelation knowledge," keep coming. (Consistently, Ginny has also gotten "revelation knowledge" regarding my life and ministry.) "You are one of the Lord's chosen vessels," Geri says under that special anointing, "God is going to use you in a mighty way."

A word given through the February Full Gospel speaker ties in. Under strong anointing, brother Thompson had pointed me out with this word (in essence): "My sister, God's anointing is upon you. You have a heart of love and compassion – unable to use it as you should – you keep thinking 'this has to happen or that has to get straightened out' before God can use you, but God would say to you, 'hold onto your hat' for He is getting ready to use you!" There was more such as, "With your hands you'll heal." Sandy, a precious sister from Golgotha, stood by. She hugged me and shared my joy.

Shortly before the second deliverance session, our household's water supply takes on an unbearably foul odor. Two men from the water company come out to give "scientific" explanation for an intolerable situation that lingers for days. Ironically, the day after the second session

– with this thing at its peak, the manager of a local religious TV program calls. He has seen my book and wants me on the program *that afternoon*. Taping is at 1:00. I have no transportation and he insists on picking me up. It sounds wonderful – a way to get my book out! The cover of beautiful flowering dogwoods would certainly be appropriate for the Easter season. There is only one hitch – a check in my spirit. Somehow, this is not God. (Ginny wholeheartedly concurs when I later share.)

Before the third session, Carl calls. The session must be postponed. Ginny and their son are very sick and Carl is fighting symptoms. Later, Ginny tells me, "The Lord must have something really big up ahead for you – we have never known such attacks."

Chapter Ten

REVELATION KNOWLEDGE

"...My burden is light." (Matthew 11:30)

Not only was the Holy Spirit shedding plenty of light upon Satan's hatred of the deliverance ministry, itself, but through much on-going revelation and confirmation, He was pinpointing other hotly contended areas having to do with deliverance, as well. Clothed in religious garb, Satan has been able to maintain a tight hold in these areas over the centuries. Tragically, as a result, multiplied millions of church-going souls will be spending eternity in hell.

A year or so before the baptism in the Spirit, the Lord began to deal with me in one of these areas. I was satisfied with the teachings of my church and discussions (arguments!) on the subject of water baptism meant little to me. But then, one day while teaching weekday school, Colossians 2:12 arrested my attention. This verse says, *"Buried with him in baptism, wherein also ye are risen with him through the faith of the operation of God, who hath raised him from the dead."* Deep within, a stirring began and, although my understanding was veiled, I started sensing that, somehow, through infant baptism, I had been cheated.

As mentioned in chapter two, the baptism in the Holy Spirit brought soul-wrenching revelation regarding the church and its unsaved multitudes who trusted a form of godliness with all its doctrines and rituals to save them. And the Lord also began to deal with me again, personally, on the subject of water baptism. The veil lifted from Colossians 2:12 and its symbolic meaning became clear. I saw that water baptism was an outward sign of salvation – that going under the waters of baptism publicly identifies the believer with Jesus in His death and burial and that coming up out of the water symbolizes his new resurrection life in Jesus and his intention to follow Him. It was clear to see why those who are saved submit themselves as soon as possible after salvation to (the humiliation of) water baptism through immersion.

Jesus' baptism (Matthew 3:16, Mark 1:9,10) and the baptism of the Ethiopian eunuch (Acts 8:35-38) gave clear evidence for immersion as the scriptural way for water baptism. Still, I asked the Lord to let me know without a shadow of a doubt what He wanted me to do. Soon, everywhere I turned, I was confronted with water baptism via immersion – *in a river,* no less! Astounded, because I'd forgotten how I had prayed, I asked the Lord if He were trying to tell me something. He reminded me of my prayer and the subject was forever settled. Later, the details for this baptism of obedience, or believer's baptism, were worked out in God's own precious way when the subject was brought up and a believer graciously offered her swimming pool. And, through a new hairdo previously acquired, I realized the Lord had even settled for me my concern (vanity!) about my appearance in public with wet hair!

My mind was at peace concerning myself long before my own water baptism took place. Still, the Holy Spirit would not let me rest. Infant baptism remained a part of Golgotha and I saw the awful confusion surrounding the subject. Did salvation depend upon infant baptism or not? Was one saved, or was he not, through this doctrine of the church? One dear soul was left in a quandary one Sunday attempting to get an answer during a group session with our elders.

Knowing that God is not the author of confusion (I Corinthians 14:33), my heart ached for poor confused souls. In addition, the Lord let me see something else that absolutely rent my heart. I noted that babies brought forward for infant baptism literally screamed their heads off. Their tender spirits seemed to be crying out in opposition! This revelation became so powerful that I felt I would become ill should I sit through one more infant baptism.

To confirm what I am sure I already knew, I had learned back before Golgotha's dedication through ladies assisting with banners that Mother Church had begun to embroider the words, "Born - Again," on the tiny (keepsake) napkins given each baby after "baptism." There was no mistaking it. Infant baptism was being equated to new birth. Most distressing was the fact that these ladies (former longtime members of Mother Church) were actually thrilled, believing Mother to be growing spiritually after the split. (We had come out of Mother, but Mother had not come out of us!)

I had been taught that the "one baptism" of Ephesians 4:5 meant infant baptism. But the Holy Spirit showed me that the one baptism mentioned here takes place at new birth when the Holy Spirit baptizes us into Jesus Christ and into His body (Romans 6:3-7, I Corinthians 12:13, and Galatians 3:27). The Holy Spirit is the agent who baptizes us into Jesus (I Corinthians 12:13) and Jesus is the agent who baptizes us in the Holy Spirit (Matthew 3:11, John 1:31-33). Glory! God alone will get the glory! For water baptism, man is the agent (Matthew 28:19).

The March 6th Men's Full Gospel breakfast meeting had been ordained of God, I knew, to bring glorious confirmation and exhortation. The speaker was Evangelist A. G. Dornfeld who had served as a Missouri Synod Lutheran pastor. Eldrin was especially thrilled to meet Rev.

Dornfeld whose book, *Have You Received the Holy Spirit?* was wonderfully used of God in my life. Returning home with great enthusiasm, Eldrin shared Rev. Dornfeld's bold, forthright testimony and, knowing the Lord had long been dealing with me on the subject, he brought home another of Rev. Dornfeld's books, *BORN AGAIN through Infant Baptism*? Rightly dividing the truth in this powerful little book, Rev. Dornfeld uses straightforward language and personal testimonies to openly expose Satan's fallacy that infant baptism (or any other mode of water baptism, for that matter) saves anyone.

Both Pastor and Wren Birdsong were baptized in the Spirit under Rev. Dornfeld's ministry yet, in spite of this fact, Rev. Dornfeld's eager desire to minister at Golgotha and Eldrin's personable persistence that he be invited to do so were steadfastly resisted by Pastor Birdsong. In fact, Golgotha's leadership avoided the Men's Full Gospel Ministry, for some unexplained reason.

Solid resistance persisted in another area. In my spirit I knew one could not talk openly about faith ministries like those through whom the Lord had literally thrown me a lifeline. Even back during the emergency room incident mentioned earlier, the Holy Spirit would not allow me to contact church leadership for prayer. Had I not heeded the Spirit's warning during that critical time in my faith walk, my own "mustard seed" of faith (crucial to the step-by-step obedience the Lord was requiring of me) would have been obliterated and the mission ahead most certainly aborted.

Gabi's words had been deposited in my spirit at one of those early Holy Ghost meetings when James 5:14 was brought up. This Scripture tells the believer to call for the elders of the church to pray for the sick. Verse 15 goes on to say, *"and the prayer of faith shall save the sick, and the Lord shall raise him up."* Recognized as one of God's choice leaders (wise as a serpent and harmless as a dove), Gabi simply said, "It's up to you to know who the elders are." Through her words, the Lord let me know right off that I must wait upon Him to direct me to those who would pray in faith for me. What valuable lessons in those early days!

In time, Golgotha's aversion to faith was confirmed. One Sunday, on our way out of church, Eldrin once again invited Pastor Birdsong to an upcoming full gospel meeting. In line behind us, a young man who had been attending Golgotha a short time overheard the invitation, got excited, and introduced himself. Later, he called. He had been trying to learn the particulars of a faith ministry the Lord was raising up in the area but to no avail. Puzzled by Golgotha's evasion of his questions and seeing a "light – something different" about us, he decided to call. Always overjoyed by what the Lord was doing anywhere, I praised God for at least some information to pass on to this young family man who obviously desired, with all his heart, to follow the Lord.

When the ecumenical conference came to town, Satan's hatred of faith was again confirmed. Large Fellowship, Golgotha's close friend, hosted the event with Golgotha in support. Full Gospel, too, was involved. Excitement swelled as invitations went out and the conference got underway. But before it was over the word got around. Faith Church, which, by now, was enjoying real growth, had been wholly excluded (to her credit, Faith showed up en masse, anyhow, despite the slight of no invitation, determined to show the love of God and to be a part of this gathering of the Body of Christ).

There is an interesting sidelight. Large Fellowship, led by a young charismatic minister, was rapidly gaining renown for its beautiful praise and worship ministry and growing phenomenally. Wanting to rejoice with everyone else over its success, I could not. We had never attended a service at

Large and didn't even know precisely where it was located, but in the spirit, I sensed foreboding heaviness. The Lord was showing me all was not well with this church.

The fruit that grew out of the ecumenical conference was not of the good sort. Having a definite check, we attended the last evening of the conference only. Later, I looked up the word, ecumenical, to find meanings like "of, or pertaining to the habited world," "universal" and "unity" – especially pertaining to the church – which only added to my unrest.

From diary notes, it was easy to see the devil's stepped-up strategy throughout the month preceding the conference. First, an article on "hyper faith" was circulated by Golgotha's elders – despite the fact that they, in no way, endorse the well-known evangelist who wrote the article! (My own faith is severely shaken as I read the article and I begin to doubt everything God has given me! What a battle rages through the night before a Word comes from the Lord early in the morning to set me free.) Next, Elder Mistik has an anything-but-edifying teaching on stewardship and the evils of riches. Then, we learn of pastor Birdsong's intense research on a well-known faith preacher accused of being a false prophet. Capping it off, Eldrin is presented with a stack of papers by (of all people) the Full Gospel president. These papers are filled with accusations against two well-know faith teachers!

With crystal clarity, the Holy Spirit sheds light on the enemy's plan to undermine personal faith. Step-by-step, the sheep are being conditioned to accept (swallow!) anything coming down the Pike through the conference speakers – or anyone else, for that matter, who might be sanctioned by church leadership. To cover his deceptive tricks (to all but the most discerning), Satan orchestrates shortly before the conference a powerful sermon on the importance of the baptism in the Holy Spirit and the power of God. Then, there is an about-face immediately following the conference with an oppressive sermon on the importance of (absolute) obedience to church leadership. This radical swinging back and forth seems, by now, to have become the norm at Golgotha. The name of the game, of course, is confusion – "Yes, you can, no, you can't." As one sister so aptly put it later, "In one breath they tell us we can go full speed ahead (believing and trusting God) and in the next they slam the brakes on."

Other conferences, like the Lutheran Charismatic conference, bring a flurry of excitement and subtle pressure to attend. How thrilling it had been to see the move of the Spirit within my own church but this is something entirely different. There is no leading, whatsoever, to attend. There is an unmistakable check, heaviness. I am beginning to see a pattern to all the Lord has been trying to show me – an age-old pattern used of the devil since earliest times. Having experienced the precious unity that is brought about by the Spirit of God, I sense another "unity" to be aware of and avoid.

With even more graphic revelation, the Lord continues to reveal how shepherdship is choking the life from Golgotha. For some time, I have been sensing, or seeing, as it were, in the spirit realm, a huge blender operating full-force over Golgotha. It is a *people blender*! It seems I can almost hear its frenzied churning as faster and faster it whirrs on its diabolical assignment to turn the people of Golgotha into one homogeneous mass. The Holy Spirit reveals its mission to do away with all unique individuality and particular giftings in the body of Christ! It's Satan's counterfeit for God's unity. How unbelievable all this is – just the opposite of Jesus' prayer to the Father in John 17:21 that we be one!

How great is my own personal struggle to steer clear of

this devilish device! At one point, I feel certain I can not hold on and the Lord sovereignly intervenes by sending Nan, one of Golgotha's visitors, who gives me (out of the blue!) an article on "members in particular." It is based on I Corinthians 12 – the chapter about the different parts of the body of Christ (and the gifts) which had so intrigued me while teaching weekday school! The article, which emphasizes the unique individuality and position of each person in the body of Christ, greatly strengthens and encourages me to stand fast. I give a copy to Judd who is also experiencing real torment in his attempts to stay free.

Throughout Scripture we find awe and joy expressed by those who have received God's life-giving, life-changing revelation. There are expressions like "joy unspeakable and full of glory" (I Peter 1:8), "the joy and rejoicing of mine heart" (Jeremiah 15:16), "sweet as honey," or, "as honey for sweetness" (Revelation 10:10, Ezekiel 3:1-3) to name a few. But also expressed is the other side. Jeremiah says, "I sat alone because of thy hand: for thou hast filled me with indignation" (Jeremiah 15:17). Ezekiel finds that upon his "roll" are written – "lamentations, and mourning, and woe" (Ezekiel 2:10) and after John tastes the honey, he says, "my belly was bitter" (Revelation 10:10).

Oh, how well I related to the joy, to the sweetness of having God's Word revealed – of being able to see into the spirit realm - of being entrusted with the light of God's holy revelation! But, oh how well I also related to the indignation, to the woe, to the bitterness (in the innermost being) which I knew to be the burden of the Lord.

At the onset of this Spirit-led walk, I had to learn the hard way that few would understand the double-edged sword, the unusual paradox of revelation – especially the burden. Attempts to share (with those I supposed would understand) were met with, "You are not to carry a burden" and Jesus said, "My yoke is easy and My burden light" (Matthew 11:30). Oppression would fall. The "sword" was being wrongly applied and used (by the enemy) against me, but I did not know how to counterattack and, finally, the Lord spoke plainly, "Keep your mouth shut – they don't understand where you're coming from."

I knew I was in the yoke with Jesus and He began to show me that His burden is indeed light – *revelation light!* The following year, this revelation of Matthew 11:30 would be precisely confirmed through a dynamic article written by one of the co-pastors at the exploding-in-the-Spirit Bellevue Assembly of God Church, Bellevue, Nebraska, which we attended while our son was stationed at Offutt Air Force Base, Omaha.

Well aware that one is held responsible and accountable before God for revelation received, my constant prayer remained, "Lord, help me to stay right in the center of your perfect will doing exactly what you would have me to do."

Chapter Eleven

OBEDIENCE IS BETTER
THAN SACRIFICE

"Behold, to obey is better than sacrifice, and to hearken than the fat of rams."

(I Samuel 15:22)

It is now June 23rd of this crucial year, 1982. I have an appointment with Pastor Birdsong. For weeks, there has been that certain inner knowing. Elder Mistik has been seen and, now, Pastor Birdsong must be presented with the words the Lord has given me including the word about the hierarchy! I will tell him I am a toe in the body of Christ. (I know this is important.) I am sure the Lord is sending me and I am sure of His timing. Still, I am very nervous. What can I expect? (In my spirit, I know I am not to be received.) Constantly, I pray to remain in the center of God's perfect will and to be a clean, clear channel (conduit!) through which His Spirit can operate.

Sherry, my niece, is spending the week with Janet. She senses my apprehension and prays for me (I later learn) as I make the appointment the day before. The girls need to borrow the car and Sherry calls back as they hurry out, "Aunt Christal, I believe I got a word from the Lord for you last night." My spirit leaps within me! I *know* she has a word! They return late and I open my Bible, quickly, to the Scriptures Sherry gives me:

"But continue thou in the things which thou hast learned and hast been assured of, *knowing of whom thou has*

learned them. "
(II Timothy 3:14, emphasis mine)

"But watch thou in all things, endure afflictions, do the work of an evangelist, *make full proof of thy ministry. "*
(II Timothy 4:5, emphasis mine)

Ah, that precious *right now* word! My inner man is instantly charged. The Lord has been disclosing that it is time for "full proof" of my ministry yet Satan's doubts assail me – "Did God really say?" And "Who are you?"! The Lord knows exactly the reinforcement needed and sends it through my precious teenage niece. She simply tells the Lord she knows I need a word from Him and is led, immediately, to these verses with no idea of how they might apply. Glory!

The session with Pastor Birdsong (amiable enough) is three hours long. Each word pertaining to my appointed place in the body of Christ is shared (the prophet's office is not to be mentioned at this time). I talk about the attack preceding ministry with the Wrenchers, Satan's hatred of deliverance and of those God wants to use. The word about the hierarchy brings no noticeable reaction. Emphasis is placed on the burden for Golgotha's deliverance and on the burning desire that we become the New Testament church God has raised us up to be.

After our meeting, Pastor Birdsong needs a ride home and as I'm pulling out of his driveway, he runs back to my car (evidently, all the talk about deliverance is getting to him). He asks me to pray for Wren, says her medication is no longer taking effect and that one side of her face is pulling down. He adds that she is not willing to receive ministry (from the Wrenchers) at this time. Later, I learn Wren shuts herself off in seclusion in her room while her family fends for itself.

A month or so before meeting with Pastor Birdsong, I

had learned of an inquiry he had made of a brother who was also led to the Wrenchers. This brother was asked if he thought the Wrenchers would teach the elders deliverance. Hope had tried to rise within me, yet I knew all was not kosher, because it is God, not man, who calls one into deliverance as well as all other ministries. And although Ginny, especially, seemed drawn in the spirit to Pastor Birdsong, nothing (to my knowledge) ever came of Pastor Birdsong's desire.

In spite of constant intercession for Wren, nothing happens. Then, at some point, I have a graphic dream in which I go to Pastor Birdsong's house to minister to Wren, but seated in the doorway to her room is Pastor Birdsong. He is reading a paper, yet I am keenly aware that he sees me and that there is no way to get beyond him to Wren! His eyes, which seemingly, see every-where, emanate something definitely not of God. The confirmation through this dream is gripping. *Pastor Birdsong, himself, is standing in the way of his wife's deliverance!*

However, there is reason for hope once again when, two Sundays after our meeting, Pastor Birdsong offers up a prayer for a New Testament church. The prayer seems taken word for word from my letter to Elder Nutral which was also shared at the meeting! We may yet become the church God wants us to be!

Hope keeps me going and, at times, my joy knows no bounds as the disbursement of *There's More to be Had* continues. It is July 23rd. Naomi and Harlan visit. They are leaving our area (and Golgotha) for Florida (after Harlan's retirement) and, en route, they plan to visit the 700 Club. Naomi asks for two signed books to take along. God is no respecter of persons, but I am so excited I have trouble making legible inscriptions in the books that will go to Pat Robertson and Ben Kinchlow of the 700 Club!

The year's events accelerate. We learn that Arnie, headed back to college, is, suddenly, without a place to live. There is pressure that he be housed with Elder Eel. There is something "kinky" about Elder Eel and Arnie is in dire straits. Janet is ready to leave for college and the Lord speaks to both Eldrin and I that Arnie is to come live with us, which he does. Later, I recall a word from the Lord that came while building our house – "This place will be a place of rest and refuge for My people passing through." The fulfillment begins!

We have special kinship with Arnie, sensing God's hand on his life. I am excited believing God is sending him to minister to Eldrin and me (we could surely use ministry). When this does not materialize, I am disappointed and the Lord lets me know He is sending Arnie to us for ministry! Quickly confirmed, the reason is straightforward, specific.

On Sunday, August 15, the day after Arnie moves in, Ariel (the saint who served with Kathryn Kuhlman) enters my life. Eldrin makes her acquaintance after church and, excitedly, brings her to meet me. It is later learned she is a widow of some years (her husband was tragically killed) yet she remains undaunted in her love for the Lord and her dedication to serve Him. She does not know why she is at Golgotha except she is going through difficult times (heavy spiritual warfare) and needs a church. She comes via Sandy and her husband, Ray, having been drawn by Ray's "Jesus" shirt while eating out! We share God's call on our lives and Ariel soberly reflects, "Maybe we are to be pillars in this church." Her words make impact.

The following Sunday, Janet leaves for college. The three-hour drive might as well be three thousand miles. For me, cutting the cords is extremely painful. We have been close. She has been my angel sent from God through the most difficult time of my life. The cup of sorrows is not over. How can I possibly make it without her? Yet, God's perfect timing is in this, too.

That week, Elna comes on the scene. Elna, fairly new at Golgotha, is acquiring a name for herself as a woman of God. How I love to be around those who hear from God, yet I know the importance of waiting on the Lord for contacts. Elna calls to say she has been "blessed – receiving confirmation" through my book. This is the first contact with Elna. Others will follow.

As though the year is not already eventful enough, the Lord will not let me off the hook regarding one of the "hotly contended areas" mentioned earlier. Under conviction day and night, I finally get up one morning in the wee hours. The words come precisely. There is an "I Wish" list that can be filled out and left in the collection plate for church leadership to review. Again, I am very nervous knowing the action about to be taken can add nothing but demerits to my already questionable popularity status. My "list" turns into this note left in the collection plate that Sunday:

"I wish that infant baptism were discontinued and replaced with infant dedication. Water baptism saves no one – neither infants nor adults – only Jesus saves. Personally, I have witnessed confusion (among Golgotha members) about what it means to be born again. The devil is the author of confusion. No one should be denied the right to his own genuine born-again experience with the Lord Jesus Christ. I have grieved in my spirit when I've seen this confusion because no one will enter heaven unless he is truly born again. I believe God, in His grace, will keep the child of dedicated Christian parents until that child can come to the place where he makes his own decision for Christ. The subject of water baptism has been laid on my heart over and over again, but since it is such a controversial subject, I have hesitated to speak out. Now, however, I feel I must do so in obedience to the Lord. Thank

you and may God bless and direct you.”

With quick follow-up (August 27), Pastor Birdsong calls to "thank" me. The Holy Ghost gives warning and my "thread of faith" (as I have come to call it) reaches for heaven. The manipulative spirit (long since discerned) is powerful. Not only is the note's vital issue (salvation) disregarded, but also the intent of the call is to get me to rethink my position. It is "suggested" I read a book on the two "schools of thought." The Lord gives strength, wisdom to mention convicting Scripture, Dornfeld's book and the simplicity of the things of the Lord (If it's complicated, it's probably not God).

Once off the phone, however, the compulsion to read the book Pastor Birdsong suggests is overwhelming. A voice says, "He is, after all, your pastor." But I hear the Lord, "How dare you even think of going back into confusion after I have brought you out!" Praise God, the subject is again settled and I have the peace (after writing the note) which comes only with obedience to the Lord.

Again, the warfare surrounding this act of obedience is horrendous. During heaviest conviction (regarding the note), we hear that our son (now based in Nebraska) has been back home, but we neither see nor hear from him and learn of his visit with relatives only after he is gone. I know this is Satan (throwing his last poisonous spears!) yet it nearly wipes me out. Then, Janet, in pre-season volleyball training, develops terribly swollen feet and ankles (this has never happened before) and our beloved old cat, Tim, must be treated for a huge abscess following a bout with an intruder. A two-page, type-written letter next arrives from a relative accusing me of division. Included are two books by the Missouri Synod against the charismatic movement! And, on the heels of all this, Eldrin gets notice that his vacations and holidays with pay are cut off and I must report for jury duty preliminaries. These are only "highlights"! No doubt about it – the enemy has been riled!

Before the Wrenchers move out of state at the end of August, there is a surprise going-away dinner in their honor. During the time to seek the Lord that follows, there is a confirmational word through Ginny (in essence): "There is someone here, close to the Lord, filled with His love – the Spirit of the Lord is in you, on you, and even coming out (as it were) through every pore of your body – you are ready to be used." No one responds and, again, I have this witness...Ginny says she feels the word is for me and also for Fran.

It is through Fran, whom I met that evening, that the dark cloud over Large Fellowship is first confirmed. My spirit stirs within me (as it always does with this type of confirmation) but the Lord cautions that a low profile is necessary while waiting on Him.

The Wrenchers' departure leaves another void and then Betty moves away also. Missing Janet terribly and desiring true friends, I struggle at a low in the valley. But once more in a precious way, the Lord intervenes. For my birthday during this time, Sunny is led to give me a particular plaque. It is shaped like a white stone and on it are written the words "I have called you, you are Mine" (Isaiah 43:1). One look and I simply melt. Not only has this Scripture been on my heart, but in addition, I have been thinking of Jesus' promise to the overcomer of a white stone whereon a new name is written (Revelation 2:17). Later, Sandy (knowing nothing of Sunny's gift) sends a birthday card with Isaiah 43:1,2 (God's promise to be with us through the fire) included in a note! Praise, God, we have a High Priest who is touched by our infirmity (Hebrews 4:15)!

There is more than warfare on the home front. Judd

and Dede, who are among others targeted, come for
fellowship and prayer. The phone rings. It is the church
leadership calling from the vicinity of Judd's house. Not
finding Judd home, they call here. (How they know he is
here, I am not sure). The call has to do with a person in
Judd's area (to whom Judd has ministered) who is causing
problems. This "brother" has been attending Golgotha. It is
demanded that Judd come home immediately to discuss this
problem. The call, which seems unreasonable (provoking
both anger and fear), is not complied with. The next day,
Pastor Birdsong and Elder Eel arrive unannounced at Judd's
to tell him he is under their authority. Dede makes an excuse
to get out of the house and calls for prayer...This thing is
becoming really heavy and I wonder how much longer it
can go on.

An oppressive sermon on submission follows. It seems
aimed, directly, at Eldrin and me and we struggle with
condemnation. To make matters worse, one of the
(previously used) "spokes" sits by me that Sunday. She keeps
asking if I am involved in this or that and why not! By now,
the Lord has me out of virtually everything seen by man
and the accuser "You're not doing anything!" tries to settle
like a plague.

For a long time, Eldrin and I have wanted (at times,
almost desperately) to leave this church. We cannot
remember when we have not had to get our spiritual food
elsewhere in order to come back in and do warfare! But the
liberty to leave is not ours. I keep hearing the voice of the
Lord, "Don't run out of this place – there is no armor for
the back"! By now, one Scripture seems a part of me –
*"Behold, to obey is better than sacrifice, and to hearken
than the fat of rams"* (I Samuel 15:22). I know only
obedience can please the Lord and this means staying to
face the devil head-on.

In the midst of the swirling warfare, on September 20, I am awakened at 5:30 a.m. with the following word for Golgotha:

"My people, you are lacking in joy...the joy of the Lord is your strength. You are lacking in joy and boldness. My word says that the righteous are as bold as a lion. My people shall be strong and do exploits. Go forward in faith and watch Me open the doors for you."

The word is given to Pastor Birdsong who reads it before the congregation. Eight days later, on September 28, at 5:30 p.m., while praying in the Spirit, another word comes for the church:

"Be strong, my people – I say unto you, be strong in the power of the Lord. Go forward and possess the land where Satan has held a stronghold for many years. Each of you has land to possess. There may appear to be giants in the land but I will be with you. Do not draw back or I will take no pleasure in you. I have raised you up for My Name's sake. There will be division. Do not be dismayed.

Did I not say, I have come not to bring peace but a sword...to set members of a household against one another? You will be misunderstood. Fear not. I will vindicate you. Put on the whole armor of God and having done all, stand. Seek not to be men pleasers. Pray much in the Spirit...listen to the voice of My Spirit and lean not unto your own understanding. I will strengthen you. I will give you My wisdom; yea, I will give you a mouth to speak."

The same word (in essence), has burned in my spirit as a personal word since the Baptism. Now, the Lord is giving it to me for his body at Golgotha! Not only has it been given to me, but for some time, it seems, the word to "possess the land" has been trumpeted like a clarion call, via other prophetic voices, throughout the body of Christ at large.

Pastor Birdsong and Elder Mistik review the word and Pastor Birdsong has me present it during the service. As it "happens," relatives of relative's relatives visit on Sunday. They ask the head usher to locate me before the service. These visitors are Lutherans excited about the move of God. They have heard of this Spirit-filled Lutheran church and they have heard of me and want copies of my book. I know all this is not coincidental and the joy of the Lord overtakes me! Later, relatives of those visiting write for a copy of my book and the prophetic word.

An ominous cloud, however, intermingles with the joy that Sunday. A young woman has been excommunicated. It is announced that morning. There is a smile on Elder Mistik's face as he reads the word the Lord gave me. Pastor Birdsong reacts similarly. Evidently, they feel this word is just for them. Pastor Birdsong even asks me to pray for the congregation's reception of the excommunication announcement. I am confused. My heart aches for the young woman and I pray for her. Yet, if stronger steps had been taken with my son...perhaps, there would not have been such heartache.

Later, we learn this is not the first such action. Behind the scenes, a brother having marital problems has been excommunicated. Having witnessed the marvelous convicting power of the Holy Spirit upon this man as he gave his life to Christ during an evangelism visit, my soul is exceedingly heavy. Still, I know there must be leadership, and I try to believe there is justification for the action taken.

On the surface, nary a ripple follows the excommunication announcement at Golgotha. But I am aware of the deep inner turmoil of at least one person – a young lady who calls so troubled she is thinking of leaving the church. Much prayer has gone up for her (via her mother's request) before she comes to Golgotha and I have seen her touched by the power of God. Her welfare is my concern, but I can only attempt to minister the love of God without taking a stand against leadership. I am aware, also, of Judd's concern. He feels the extreme action taken can serve only to hinder others from receiving Christ.

While all appears to go along "business as usual" at Golgotha, I sense in the spirit that things are "revving up." From here on out, I know the warfare can only intensify with but one direction for me – straight ahead in obedience to God.

Chapter Twelve

AS A NAIL
FASTENED IN A SURE PLACE

"And I will fasten...as a nail in a sure place."
(Isaiah 22:23)

While things are revving up in the spirit realm, 1982 is beginning to wind down. It is Sunday, October 31st, Ariel and I are brought together after church for a divine appointment. Ariel expresses need for continued prayer. Ministry and sharing follow. Then, under the unction of the Spirit, I find myself sharing the deliverance burden, my position as a "toe" in the body of Christ and the word through Ginny that God has placed me in the center of the "wheel" at Golgotha.

As I talk, Ariel closes her eyes and begins to sway, gently, back and forth in the Spirit. Quietly, we wait upon the Lord. Something is about to come forth. What Ariel gets is not complete but she mentions Ezekiel's vision and the Spirit within the wheel. She tells me I am as a wheel within the wheel. God's sovereign presence hovers about us. I recall the ability "to see with the eye of the Spirit" into the internal affairs of the church. Burning intensely in my spirit is that very certain identity with God's prophets of old...

Ariel continues to seek the Lord and calls that afternoon. "You will be a tower of strength and authority in an end-time ministry," she says, confirming (unknown to her) a word previously given. (A week later, this word is again confirmed.) She mentions that the toe is a terminal part of the body (Daniel 2;40-44) and that Aaron was anointed on the ear, thumb and toe (Exodus 29:20). She tells me to read Ezekiel's vision of the wheel (Ezekiel 1:15-28 and Ezekiel 10) and concludes by saying she believes God will give deeper revelation of what He is trying to show me.

The Lord continues to deal with Ariel and on Friday, November 5th, she calls again. On Monday she was led to take a drive alone in her car to pray for me and over the Scriptures given. During her time away (between two and three hours), she is given a vision where I am kneeling in prayer on the seat beside her. A brilliant beam floods down over me from heaven. Becoming as one with me in this vision, Ariel is shown I am in a learning process – being refined as silver and gold...

Then comes the first of two confirmations (through anointed servants) the Lord knows will be absolutely necessary for the days ahead. "Has the Lord ever shown you He is calling you into the prophet's office?" Ariel asks. "Yes!!" I gasp reaching for pen and pad to document all that is coming through this precious yielded vessel. "The Lord has shown me this is your office," she continues. "It will be a lonely walk – set apart – much of the time you will walk entirely alone except for your husband"...By now, I am weeping profusely as God's holiness envelops me like a cloud. The Lord has already shown me each of these things none of which has been shared with Ariel. Some has not been easy to accept.

Ariel is not finished. She has also been led to James 3 which has to do with the untamed tongue – "an unruly evil, full of deadly poison" (v:8). She has been shown that tongues will come against me but reaffirms that the Lord will be with me. There is a final word. "Get the Word into your heart," she exhorts, "and, when people ask you to do something, tell them you will pray about it letting your answer be 'yea' or 'nay' according to the Lord's instruction. There is no need for any other explanation."

Following up, Ariel diligently prepares a list of Scriptures having to do with the description and function of a prophet. The Lord has already directed me to most of these.

During the week, Sandy and Ray call and come for fellowship and prayer (consistently, doors open for ministry and I remain amazed and thrilled to be used of the Lord). Sandy shares with Pastor Birdsong that some deliverance definitely took place during the evening.

That Sunday's sermon seems connected. In it we are exhorted to "enter in and receive God's gifts" and to "hear the sound of the trumpet in these last days"! Encouragement wanes quickly, however, when, during the week, it is learned that Judd continues to suffer on-going harassment. Repeatedly, Elder Eel (seemingly, bent on Judd's "undoing") calls Judd to let him know the elders will need "to see him again." Judd requests Elders Mystik, Nutral, and Ire, but Elder Eel insists that the meeting will be with him, Pastor Birdsong and Elder Thair. Surely, a snare is being laid.

Needed encouragement comes that Saturday evening through the Full Gospel speaker, Rev. A.G. Dornfeld. Pastor Dornfeld's boldness and wry humor (he got the "left foot of fellowship" after receiving the baptism in the Holy Spirit") left Eldrin chuckling for days after the men's Full Gospel breakfast and, now, I too, have a chance to hear him. We are privileged to have Pastor Dornfeld as an overnight guest realizing only later the on-going fulfillment of the word of the Lord concerning our home.

During that same day (November 13) I receive this *rhema* word from the Lord: "I am enlarging your vision, your tabernacle." As I seek the Lord I am given to know this word has to do with my sphere of influence for His kingdom and for His glory (see Isaiah 54:2,3 and Psalm

119:32).

On the evening of Judd's meeting (November 19), I maintain a three-hour prayer vigil and the message that Sunday (November 21) seems to indicate a breakthrough. Seemingly, all stops are pulled out. YES, we can go forward! YES, we can trust God and His Word! Later, I learn that the meeting with Judd had lasted until 1:30 a.m. with the leadership discussing with Judd where Golgotha is going!

The following Sunday, however, the pendulum swings back the other way. The sermon, which is heavily authoritarian and oppressive, seems aimed, directly at Judd. Throughout the week, spiritual warfare seems to reach an all-time high and discouragement all but swallows me up.

On Sunday, December 12, I have the glorious Holy Ghost camp meeting with Ariel already covered in Chapter three. As though this were not enough – and with the word from the Lord through Ariel (October 31 and November 5) still burning like a fire in my spirit, I see Geri! She is again visiting her daughter and back at Golgotha. We come together for another of those divine appointments and for the second powerful word of confirmation the Lord knows I will need.

Geri reads the two prophetic words the Lord has given me for Golgotha which are kept handy in my Bible. She tells me she has shared with her daughter and son-in-law that the Lord has placed me in the prophet's office, but that I am not only unrecognized by Golgotha's leadership, but actually shunned! She then tells me God is going to send me before the leadership with a word, but that they will receive neither me, nor the word! Nothing of what the Lord has been showing me about going before leadership with a word has ever been shared with Geri. This thing will be coming to pass, but when and how and what is the word?

The New Year, 1983, comes in with some of the heaviest

oppression I have known. I call Ariel for prayer. She ministers and prays and asks the Lord to show me in a special way that He loves me and is with me. Later, in my prayer closet, I glance up through the window to see a beautiful rainbow covering half the sun and, with astonishment, I recall Ariel's prayer and know this is surely a precious sign from the Lord to me.

The Lord continues to give an even deeper awareness of the need for deliverance at Golgotha and within the Body of Christ at Large. On January 26, Brad calls for ministry and prayer that lasts for two hours (the Lord had previously shown me the need for deliverance in his family). The counterattack that follows is such that I go to bed with severe headache and nausea. The next day I am totally well! That Sunday, Brad shares with me that everything turned around for the better after the ministry and prayer. All praise to God!

Confirmation continues to come regarding the ungodly shepherdship that is tightening its noose around Golgotha. There is now talk of "under-shepherds" who will assist the shepherds (pastors and elders) in exercising control over the sheep.

Under the leadership of the Holy Spirit, I call Pastor Birdsong, February 8, to have an announcement put in the church bulletin on an upcoming meeting with Pastor Dornfeld ministering in our home. Immediately, I sense resistance. "Pastor Dornfeld is too bold, too dogmatic ...we don't want to blow the sheep away."

Leaning again very heavily on the Lord for wisdom, I tell him we really feel the Lord has opened the door for this meeting and ask for prayer on how we are to get the word out and that the Lord will send the people He wants to the meeting. I then tell pastor Birdsong of Pastor Dornfeld's son-in-law who is home for Christmas, sees my book, reads it once, then twice, gets all excited and says, "this book needs to be in the hands of every Lutheran Pastor!" Pastor Birdsong makes no comment, but tells me he will bring up the home meeting when the elders meet tonight and will call me back tomorrow.

February 9, Pastor Birdsong calls back to say the elders agreed we can have the home meeting and that we can invite people on an individual basis. However, "if Dornfeld gets too bold, you and Eldrin are to call him aside and get him in line." No announcement of the meeting will be made in the church bulletin and we, of course, are not to make an announcement, publicly, at church.

On February 18, the meeting with Pastor Dornfeld is held in our home. It is a small meeting, but we are blessed. During the meeting, Pastor Dornfeld looks around at the fifteen or so people gathered and says, "This is the way we will be meeting before the Lord's return (in homes.)" Mrs. Dornfeld prophesies of the Lord's very soon return. Pastor and Mrs. Dornfeld spend the night and the next morning at breakfast, Pastor Dornfeld says there is heavy oppression at Golgotha and indicates we need to get out. We nod, but tell him the Lord won't let us go. With that, this dear elderly saint of God looks at us intently, then simply raises his eyes to heaven and says, "Lord forgive me," (for giving up perhaps too quickly on the Lutheran Church). We share nothing of what has been taking place at Golgotha nor of what our assignment is to be.

Sunday, February 20, Pastor Birdsong speaks forth during his sermon with the most brazen and oppressive statements to be heard thus far, "There are people who are always talking about revelation knowledge; if you can get revelation knowledge directly from God, there would be no need of leadership...these people have independent spirits and the devil will pick them off." Fear tactics are now being used in an even greater degree to prevent the sheep from seeking and hearing directly from God. Quickly, for future reference, I jot down on the back of my bulletin what has just been said. I know, via the Holy Spirit, that these words are aimed directly at me and the attack is so great that I want the floor to open and swallow me up.

These words bother me so much that I finally call Ariel. She too, has been troubled and approached Pastor Birdsong. He gives some sort of explanation brushing it aside and it is dismissed. But the Lord will not let me dismiss what I have heard. It is one of the strongest confirmations to date of the devil's intent to rob the sheep of their most sacred privilege, the right to hear directly from the Shepherd – Jesus! – for themselves.

Interestingly enough, Brad, who has recently gotten ministry and a tremendous release within his family, comes to me after the February 20 service to tell me Ariel has a "rebellious" spirit. I cannot believe my ears! There is not a rebellious bone in this godly woman's body. I listen cautioned of the Spirit to say nothing and to keep all I have heard to myself. Later, it is learned that Brad is being considered for an "under-shepherd" role. Ariel is called rebellious because she opts to wait upon God for employment in her specialized field rather than succumbing to the advice of the leadership that she get a fast food job.

The great paradox of my life continues. On the one hand there is this ongoing fiery trial and, on the other hand, God's wonderful blessings continue. The Lord has shown me that the fiery trial would lose its power after two events have occurred. First, "There's More to be Had" would need to be published which, of course, has taken place and, secondly, there would need to be a significant spiritual turn around in the life of my son. I sensed that the second event was not too far down the road.

Our son, Mitch, is now stationed at SAC Head-quarters in Omaha, Nebraska and on March 6, we are blessed beyond words when we visit him and his wife. Mary, and attend the "exploding in the Spirit" Bellevue Assembly of God church that they have attended a time or two.

The night before, I have a deep spiritual longing that Mitch and Mary develop a hunger for spiritual things and be filled with the Spirit. Fervently, I have been praying along this line. So as Mitch and his dad work on repairing a radio the evening before, I pull down a Bible from a nearby shelf and open to Acts Two. Mitch asks what I'm reading and chuckles with acknowledgment when I say, "Acts chapter two." Nothing more is said on the subject.

The next morning at breakfast, I am asked to say the prayer. Later, I see God's hand in all of this. My heart's cry is that the message at the church that morning be especially geared to Mitch and Mary and aloud I pray that it might have to do with the need for God's Spirit in this final hour.

When the Church's senior pastor, Sam Mayo, gets up that morning to deliver his message, he says the Lord will not allow him to continue with "Principles of Kingdom Living" as planned. His message is on *Acts Chapter Two and the need to receive the power of the Holy Spirit in this final hour!*

We have to leave before the service is over to tour the underground SAC Headquarters as planned, but Eldrin shares later that Mary raises her hand when the invitation is given for those who would like to receive the Holy Spirit. Our children cannot but see the hand of God in the change of message that morning. I am astounded at the Lord's faithfulness and goodness. We leave a back-masking tape that fully exposes the devil in rock music and, after hearing it, Mitch destroys his large collection of hard rock records. Glory!

As expected, following the blessing of March 6, the backlash of the enemy is horrendous. On March 10, Ariel calls. As she is praising the Lord, I come before her. The Lord shares His love for me with her – lets her know I am as the woman with the alabaster box of precious ointment which she pours over Jesus' head (Matthew 26:6-13). Once before a similar word had been given and in the future, it will be given again. The Lord knows I need this encouragement!

They've heard about my book, *There's More to be Had,* and I am asked to speak at a small church in the town where I attended high school. The week before I am hit in the back, suddenly, violently, and without warning. I am enduring excruciating pain. I know the attack is directly connected with the speaking engagement. We bind Satan's power and stand on the Word. After church on April 10, I get prayer for the meeting from one of the elders upon whom I had once sensed the anointing. Much to my dismay, he prays that the Lord will put a guard over my mouth! I am needing boldness and he prays that the Lord will put a guard over my mouth (I am still trying to do the "right" thing by submitting to leadership)! This man's wife, however, seems to be in a different camp. As she lays hands on my lower back and prays, I feel intense heat. Afterwards, she shares that, during the prayer, she saw a bright, almost blinding light.

Then, I see Geri, who is back at Golgotha. She gives the devil more than a "black eye" as she prays for me and the meeting and, Praise God, this prayer undoes the effects of the elder's prayer! I go that evening wearing a back support and low-heeled shoes and speak for almost two hours under God's anointing. I share the oppression the Lord has allowed me to sense over that area and the burden He has given me for it. What a blessing it is to see the power and moving of the Holy Spirit as people fall to their knees praying and weeping before God.

That afternoon, as I was praying and standing against the spirit of fear trying to immobilize me (I had not spoken much and it would be especially difficult to speak in home territory), the Lord spoke plainly, "Think in terms of eternity." Only the hereafter can reveal how our obedience to God has affected the lives of people for all eternity.

On April 14, the word, "LACHISH," keeps coming to me strongly in a vision through the night hours. It is spelled out in large capital letters. When I get up the next morning the word is forgotten, until I have my Bible reading for the day. There, in II Kings 18:17, the word "Lachish," nearly jumps off the page at me! The Lord instructs me to look up the word in my Bible dictionary. Thus, it read: "Canaanite royal city and *Judean border fortress occupying a strategic valley* 25 miles Southwest of Jerusalem (emphasis mine)." Once again, the Spirit of God envelops me as a cloud. He lets me know I am as a border fortress located in a strategic place at Golgotha for the protection of His people! I think of how this latest word ties in with the word "conduit," and it's second meaning "protector."

At the end of April, Judd comes for prayer. He is under heavy oppression. It is such that he can hardly talk. By submitting to leadership in a certain situation, he knows he has disobeyed God. As I wait on the Lord, suddenly, out of my mouth come these words. **"The Lord is my Shepherd, no shepherd is my Lord**." *I see this word, go into Judd's Spirit*! The day or so before, I had heard a minister speak forth these words on Christian TV and now the Holy Spirit recalls them for Judd! He is set totally free.

We are now in the month of May, I learn Judd and Dede have left Golgotha. I am saddened, but know there is no recourse. The harassment and suppression have been too great. Sylvester is a good friend of Judd and Dede's. He is a godly man who has been used in my life, along with Judd and Dede, to bring encouragement and a word in due season. I am glad he, too, did not leave Golgotha.

By June, Mitch is transferred to Goodfellow AFB, Texas, and there, at Christ the King church, under the precious leadership of Pastor Perry and Glory Griffith, he and Mary are placed in a spiritual hothouse where they receive the baptism of the Spirit and the power of God. Hallelujah!

Just as the Lord has shown me He is about to do a deeper work in my son, He is now showing me that the assignment at Golgotha is close at hand. According to God's perfect timing, *the two will coincide.*

The zeal of the Lord burns with even greater intensity within me. Three Scriptures the Lord gave me soon after receiving the power of God summarized my life at this time. John the Baptist had cried out, *"Repent ye: for the kingdom of heaven is at hand. For this is He that was spoken of by the prophet Esaias, saying, the voice of one crying in the wilderness, prepare ye the way of the Lord, make his paths straight"* (Matthew 3:3 and Isaiah 40:3). He had also given me Jeremiah 20:9, *"His word was in mine heart as a burning fire shut up in my bones...and I could not stay"* plus *"The zeal of thine house hath eaten me up"* (consumed me) (Psalm 69:9 and John 2:17). How well I understand these Scriptures and know that, even as God had called these servants to cry out, He has called me.

Two of the leaders, especially, have been pinpointed as exercising manipulative control. Am I to go to just these two? But the Lord continues to show me, as in a vision, that I will go before the entire leadership. I see myself before them and I can hear what I will say. The Lord has shown me that neither I, nor the word will be received and, in addition, that we will be "crucified" in that church. It is a fearsome and awesome thing. The Lord really "nailed" down this assignment with the most recent word through Geri, yet, in spite of all the other words of confirmation, I continue to cry out with fear and trembling before the Lord. He is so gracious and merciful letting me know the words He has given me are "as a nail fastened in a sure place" (Isaiah 22:23), and that I must hold onto them until further instruction comes from His heavenly throne room.

Chapter Thirteen

STAND FAST IN LIBERTY!

"Stand fast therefore in the liberty wherewith Christ hath made us free. And be not entangled again with the yoke of bondage."

(Galatians5:1)

Once, I had heard Kenneth Copeland say that when God got his big machine in gear, he wanted to be right up on the front end of that thing. I too, although fearful and trembling, felt exactly the same way. Now, via the mighty Holy Spirit of God, I know that God's big machine is in high gear and ready to roll at Golgotha. I also know, by the Holy Spirit that I am right up on the front end of that thing!

I had been up in the face of God. Before me I held a note containing Geri's word that I would be sent before leadership with a word, but that neither the word nor I would be received. I tell the Lord that I know Geri is His servant and that the word she had given was simply confirmation of the word He had already given me. I then said, "Lord, if this is so, please bring this thing to pass quickly."

On June 26 Elna calls. God's big machine has begun to roll! Elna tells me that Ricky (a godly man) had been led to talk with her that morning at church. He said he felt that those of us to whom the Lord had given revelation concerning leadership should get together and pray. Elna tells me that the Lord has shown her that we are generals in His army and that we are to keep confidential within our ranks what the Lord shows us. She feels, as I, that Golgotha is at a crossroads and that something is about to take place.

I share with Elna how the Lord has shown me He will send me before leadership with a word. I also share how, through a prophetic word, I have been shown that soon I will be taken from the middle. She says the Lord has spoken virtually that same thing to her and that she was sent to Golgotha to "lead God's people (as Moses) to the Promised Land." She said she would then be free (to lead). She said the Lord had shown her that after the breakthrough with leadership, I, too, would be free. I didn't know what all this meant, but it sounded good!

The next evening, a meeting is held in our home. Present are Elna and her husband, Gary, Ricky, Eldrin and I and Arnie. We are awed as we share, by the confirmation given to each of us through the others who have received the same thing! We all feel the Lord is showing us that the main problem at Golgotha is coming through two of the leaders – Pastor Birdsong and Elder Eel – each operating under a strong spirit of manipulation which has fallen over onto the rest. As a result, I mention that the sheep are being hurt and even destroyed (over and over, I've heard the Lord saying, "My sheep are languishing." I look up the work languish. It means among other things, "to be weak, to lose strength, to waste away with longing").

I share how the Lord has shown me that Pastor Birdsong is standing squarely in the way of his wife's deliverance. This is confirmed, emphatically, by Gary who also confirms a number of other things I feel led to share. Arnie shares how he has been given a vision of a train (Golgotha) racing full-speed down the track to destruction.

After this time of sharing and confirmation, we pray and wait on the Lord to show us how to proceed. I share how I feel the Lord wants Gary to go forth as our spokesman, but that, eventually, we all will go before leadership for questioning. This is confirmed by the rest. Gary is to present only this word at the initial meeting: "The enemy is among you."

During the day, Elna said the Lord had given her this word for our prayer group:

> *"O, my children, the separation is beginning but, beware, the enemy is among you. He is like a wolf in sheep's clothing ready to devour you. You must be on your guard. Put on the full armor of God. Test the spirits, test the teachers, test the prophets. Test them by my Word. My Word is your sword. Learn to use it. Learn to wield it. Fear not the enemy for I have overcome the enemy. Look to me for your strength. I will be with you. The battle has been won. Claim the victory."*

Earlier that evening, Elna and I had talked about our call to the prophet's office and how we both felt fearful and inadequate for the calling. At one point, Elna mentions that both she and I are as Moses to lead the people of Golgotha up to the promised land and that they (the leadership) will come after us, but not Ricky because he would be as Joshua to lead the people in. I could sense the severity of what was just ahead and praised the Lord for raising up Elna and Ricky. I would not have to go alone before leadership as I thought so surely the Lord had shown me!

By now, the sheep of Golgotha are ripe for deliverance and freedom. The Lord shows me He has used the years of intercession to open their hearts and bring this about. But there remains the problem that grows increasingly worse. Throughout the month of June and during the weeks to follow, the Lord brings one confirmation after another regarding the abusive, controlling power of the leadership that is being exercised over weak and wounded sheep. Once again, and over and over, I get another word from the Lord; "They will not let my people enter in!" I look up the Scripture in its entirety:

> *"Woe unto you, scribes and Pharisees, hypocrites! For ye*
> *shut up the kingdom of heaven against men: for ye neither*
> *go in yourselves, neither suffer ye them that are entering*
> *to go in."*
>
> *(Matthew 23:13)*

On June 29, Melanie calls. We go to the same church, but have never met, nor talked. I only know who she is and that her husband is a doctor. For weeks, Melanie says the Lord has been putting me very strongly on her heart and that she has tried many times to reach me. By now, our phone has begun to ring all too frequently and, at times, we simply take it off the hook trusting God to make the connections He wants.

Melanie has seen a copy of *There's More to be Had* (to be given to someone) under my chair during a recent church service and her spirit had been greatly quickened. We talk about the book and she asks if the Lord has called me into a healing ministry. She says she has been diagnosed with an incurable disease, which she does not accept as incurable since receiving the power of God.

I tell Melanie the Lord has used me in healing a few times and recount the burning desire after the Baptism in the Spirit to lay hands on the sick and simply say, "In the name of Jesus, be healed" (later, I also recall the word through Brother Thompson, "with your hands you'll heal"). But laying hands on Melanie or even praying for her for healing is not God's purpose at this time. Melanie says that for some reason, she knows we will need to get together in person. That meeting occurs the following Sunday, July 3, after church. Melanie tells me she has talked with a certain elder. She tells him I have a part of something God is doing at Golgotha, which also includes him. It is amazing to see the insight of God's people and how they are used to bring confirmation!

Beginning that Sunday, July 3, the Lord proceeds to fasten His "nails" in a sure place in another exciting way – *up from the cover of the church bulletin*. Prior to that time, it is doubtful I had ever really noticed the cover of a church bulletin but, now the words literally lift from the page to become a *rhema* word of confirmation/instruction on a regular basis until we are finally expelled from the church.

There is a story that ties in with the first word to be given in this fashion. In 1978, we had visited Heritage USA and, there, in the little gift shop just opening I had purchased a pair of plaques. One contained the words, "Jesus is Lord" which thrilled me to no end. The other, however, contained a Scripture I did not understand at the time and would not have purchased had it not made a matching pair. God had His own plan and perfect timing for that second plaque!

For days, perhaps weeks, my attention has been directed to this second plaque with it's Scripture now made very clear: *"Stand fast therefore in the liberty wherewith Christ hath made us free" (Galatians 5:1)*. The word that meets me from the church bulletin on July 3 is the second half of this Scripture, *"Do not submit again to a yoke of slavery"* (Galatians 5:1, RSV). Each part of the Scripture could stand alone for they have basically the same meaning.

In addition, the Lord has been directing my attention to Galatians 3:1,3, which states, *"Oh foolish Galatians, who hath bewitched you...Are ye so foolish? Having begun in the Spirit, are you now made perfect by the flesh?"* I know that we at Golgotha, like the foolish Galatians, who had started in the Spirit, have now gone back to the flesh, back under a yoke of bondage, back under the law, legalism...death.

Elna calls again on July 6, Gary did not get to deliver

his message at the council meeting the night before as planned since only three leaders were present. His meeting with leadership is rescheduled for the following Saturday morning. Once again, Elna and I compare notes as to what the Lord has been giving us. Gary had been given a Scripture that he had shared with the group last Monday evening. I had failed to write it down and Elna reiterates:

> *"And that because of false brethren unawares brought in, who came in privily to spy out our liberty which we have in Christ Jesus, that they might bring us into bondage."*
> *(Galatians 2:4)*

As a directive, and as confirmation on the procedure we are taking, Elna had gotten this word:

> *"Against an elder receive not an accusation, but before two or three witnesses."*   *(I Timothy 5:19)*

Elna had also been led to I Timothy1:3-11, which has to do with teachers getting into the law, rather than godly edifying. Then, Elna said that yesterday, she had gotten a copy of the June issue of *Believer's Voice of Victory* magazine. She wanted to know if I had seen the magazine and if I had read Kenneth Copeland's prophecy to the shepherds contained therein.

"Yes!" I told Elna, hardly able to believe my ears. The Lord, seemingly, had us on the same spiritual wave length and now, this latest confirmation though Kenneth Copeland! We were not as yet on Kenneth Copeland's mailing list, but someone had sent the magazine through the mail calling my attention to the prophetic word. It was a strong message to the shepherds, warning them to stop devouring the sheep and one another and to stop resisting the mighty move of the Spirit of God.

The confirmation that had come through this prophetic word was *profound, unmistakable*. Some time prior to receiving the magazine, I had been very diligently seeking the Lord for the word he would have me give the shepherds of Golgotha. I was given "feed my sheep!" It was the title of Chapter 26 in *There's More to be Had*. The word was succinct, final. There would be no more seeking the Lord on this matter. Along with this brief word, I must also give them Jeremiah 23:1-4, which the Lord had instructed me to include in that chapter:

> "Woe be unto the pastors that destroy and scatter the sheep of my pasture! saith the Lord. Therefore, thus saith the Lord God of Israel against the pastors that feed my people; Ye have scattered my flock, and driven them away, and have not visited them; behold, I will visit upon you the evil of your doings, saith the Lord. And I will gather the remnant of my flock out of all countries whither I have driven them, and will bring them again to their folds; and they shall be fruitful and increase. *And I will set up shepherds over them which shall feed them; and they shall fear no more, nor be dismayed, neither shall they be lacking, saith the Lord"*
>
> (Jeremiah 23:1-4, my emphasis)

At the time this was given, I thought it was a word just for pastors in the traditional church who were resisting the move of the Holy Spirit. It was, indeed, for them, but now I know, with certainty, this is the word of the Lord that must be given Golgotha's leadership.

When I tell Elna that this will be a hard word to give, she says, "wait until you hear what the Lord has given me!" She had gotten Ezekiel 34 - the entire chapter but, for brevity's sake, only the following will be listed here:

> *"Son of man, prophesy against the shepherds of Israel,*

prophesy, and say unto them. "Thus saith the Lord God unto the shepherds; Woe be to the shepherds of Israel that do feed themselves! Should not the shepherds feed the flocks? Ye eat the fat, and ye clothe you with the wool, ye kill them that are fed; but ye feed not the flock. The diseased have ye not strengthened, neither have ye healed that which was sick, neither have ye bound up that which was broken, neither have ye brought again that which was driven away, neither have ye sought that which was lost; but with force and with cruelty have ye ruled them. And they were scattered, because there is no shepherd: and they became meat to all the beasts of the field, when they were scattered. Therefore, O ye shepherds, hear the word of the Lord; thus saith the Lord God; Behold, I am against the shepherds; and I will require my flock at their hand, and cause them to cease from feeding the flock; neither shall the shepherds feed themselves any more; for I will deliver my flock from their mouth, that they may not be meat for them."

(Ezekiel 34:2-5,9,10)

It is indeed an even harder word and one I am glad I won't have to give! But that is as far "off the hook" as I am going to get.

That evening as I pick up an old study Bible to again review Ezekiel 34, this note meets me from the margin on the opposite page: *"If you do not warn the wicked of his way, he will die in his iniquity, but his blood will I require at their hand"* (Ezekiel 33:8 in my own words).

It was a word the Lord had given me in 1981. There was no choice but to obey! This word had been before me strongly along with these Scriptures the Lord had also given at that time:

"Have not I commanded thee? Be strong and of good courage; be not afraid, neither be thou dismayed: for the Lord thy God is with thee whithersoever thou goest."

(Joshua 1:9)

Then said I, Ah, Lord God! Behold, I cannot speak: for I am a child. But the Lord said unto me, Say not, I am a child: for thou shall go to all that I shall send thee, and whatsoever I command thee thou shalt speak. Be not afraid of their faces: for I am with thee to deliver thee, saith the Lord. Thou therefore gird up thy loins, and arise, and speak unto them all that I command thee: be not dismayed at their faces, lest I confound thee before them." (Jeremiah 1:6,7,8,17)

These Scriptures have to do with being courageous in the face of man. The Lord had confirmed my calling in no uncertain terms, he had confirmed the ungodly shepherdship at Golgotha in no uncertain terms; He has confirmed the word to be given the shepherds in no uncertain terms and, now, in no uncertain terms, He is giving final instructions. I have the very strong inner witness that before it's all over, "stand fast in liberty" will be the most crucial instruction we will have to follow.

Chapter Fourteen

AS LAMBS AMONG WOLVES

"Behold, I send you forth as lambs among wolves."
(Luke 10:3)

On July 7, my spirit is greatly quickened by this word that comes through my devotional reading: "Break loose the fetters – behold, with a strong and mighty hand will I bring my people out!"

How wonderful, I thought, God is surely going to deliver his people! And yet, in spite of all the Lord has shown me, I wonder how this is going to be accomplished. I continue to pray diligently for the church leadership hoping even at this late hour there will be a turn around and that the hearts of the leadership will be changed. I know it is of utmost importance that my own heart be clean and I have never stopped praying, "Oh God – make me a clean, clear vessel through which your Spirit can flow."

Then on Sunday, July 10, up from the cover of the church bulletin comes this sobering word: "*I send you out as lambs in the midst of wolves*" (Luke 10:3, RSV). I know this is a forewarning – one that sends shivers up and down my spine. What I sense in my spirit is definitely not a change of heart in the leadership.

Finally the day arrives! It is Tuesday, July 12. We meet at Gary and Elna's to pray for Gary as he meets with leadership to present the word. There has been a change in the word to be given. It is now, "The enemy is one of you." (I do not understand, but must trust the Lord.) At approximately 8:30 p.m. both Ricky and I get a special burden for Gary and learn when he returns that it was at that time he was about to be "chewed up and spit out" by leadership! He said his words were twisted and what he said seemed to be of no avail whatsoever. They kept insisting that he tell them who among them had been found in sin and tried to apply the principle of Matthew 18:15-17 which has to do with going alone to a brother who has offended you then taking two or more witnesses and, finally, taking the matter before the church.

As we pray and seek the Lord about what to do next, both Elna and I are strongly impressed that Gary is now to call and give the word from Ezekiel 34 and Jeremiah 23. He does so and shortly afterward Pastor Birdsong calls back. They will be right out!

It is a long evening that lasts until 2:30 a.m. We have been led to fast and pray ahead of time for this meeting. However, we learn that prior to the meeting, the Lord had spoken to each of us and said, *"Eat, you will need your strength tonight."*

To relate all that transpired during that four to five hour session would be, I believe, impossible. Much was brought into the open and discussed, yet we felt very strongly that little, if anything, we said was being received. Pastor Birdsong attempted very carefully to control and manipulate the entire evening and it seemed there was a genuine effort on the part of everyone to subvert everything we said. There was a time when I felt almost overwhelmed by the futility of what was taking place and wanted to leave it all behind *forever*. Later, Gary shared that he felt like saying, "Gentlemen, this is useless; there is the door!" Elna said she felt like getting up and running out, but then remembered it was her house!

During the evening we shared how the Lord had recently brought us together to seek Him and to pray – how Elna had received the word from Ezekiel 34 and I was given "feed my sheep" and Jeremiah 23:1-4. Kenneth Copeland's prophetic word was brought up and how the Lord had gotten the June issue of *Believers Voice of Victory* magazine into our hands. We mentioned that the word through Kenneth Copeland had precisely confirmed what the Lord had already given us for Golgotha's leadership. The word of warning from Ezekiel 33:8 is presented – "*If thou dost not speak to warn the wicked from his way...his blood will I require at thine hand.*"

Elna mentions that the preaching and teaching of Golgotha's leaders is falling more and more under the law with its heaviness rather than new covenant grace. She also tells Pastor Birdsong that his sermons are consisting more and more of quotations from books written by man rather than from the Word of God. This seems to upset him and he denies that it is so.

I share how the Lord had spoken to me in late summer or fall of 1982 that the devil was trying to raise up a "hierarchy" among leadership at Golgotha and that this word was quickly and powerfully confirmed through two sources. We tell them we feel this hierarchical stronghold had centered over Elder Eel and Pastor Birdsong, but had permeated the entire group. This ungodly shepherdship, we say, is designed to prevent the sheep from hearing directly for themselves the voice of Jesus.

Under God's anointing, I find myself actually speaking forth those things I had heard myself saying as in a vision for at least two years. Much had already been shared – first with elder Mistik and then with Pastor Birdsong. Nothing had been done in a corner. I am now at liberty to tell pastor Birdsong ((among other things) that the Lord has shown me he is standing squarely in the way of his wife's deliverance. Not once do I come under confusion or fear. I know this is God's hour to shine! It is His perfect timing!

Elder Mistik says at one point that I seem to be defending my position. I tell him Jesus has told me I am not to defend myself – that He, Himself, will be my defense. If I appear to be defensive, I say, it is for the sheep. I tell him *I am defensive of the sheep because that is where the Lord has placed me!*

As I speak, the Lord will not allow me to look at Elder Ire. I obey the Lord who shows me this man is filled with hot anger against us – how dare we (mere lay people) approach the leadership in this manner? Later, one of the members who is trying to get to the bottom of all that happened calls me. She and her husband had met with leadership and she said one of the elders did admit to having tremendous anger against us. I told her the Lord was showing me who she was talking about and mentioned his name. She was astounded and, hopefully, would begin to see that what had taken place with leadership was God ordained.

On that notable evening, Elna brings up how both Pastor Birdsong and Elder Mistik in the presence of her husband, Gary, had confirmed her calling to the prophet's office. However, at this confrontation, they excuse the whole thing saying they do not remember.

As for me, they say my calling is not accepted, because it has not been tested, and because I do not stand up and prophesy in church. Neither of these statements is true. The Lord, Himself, had put me through a grueling time of testing, training and grooming, and in September of 1982, I had been given prophetic words for the church which the leadership was well aware of.

The devil makes a grand attempt during the evening to sweep us off course by posing the question through Pastor Birdsong, "What can we do – what new programs can we introduce – to improve Golgotha?" One of our group almost falls into that trap, but the Lord has His hand on the meeting and we quickly get back to His business.

Other than Pastor Birdsong's disagreement with Elna over the content of his sermons, there is no noticeable reaction that evening to anything we say. At one point, I say, "I have the feeling that nothing we're saying is being received." Elna agrees. The leadership is silent.

Both Elna and I beg the leadership to take the word that has been given to them and go seek the Lord, fast, pray, do whatever is necessary to hear from Him on this. But they seem not to hear us. We mention how we know the severity and hardness of the word and how quickly God could bring us under judgment should we be speaking for ourselves and not for Him.

Toward the end of the session, Pastor Birdsong asks a pointed question, "Do you think Elder Eel has demons?" I sense a trap! Our group is silent and then Elna speaks out, "Either he has demons or he is demon possessed." Awestruck, I stare at Elna in disbelief. I might have thought it, but *never* would I have said it. Later, these words are attributed not to Elna, but to me!

The next day a word comes from the Lord to me. It is brief, clear, *final*. These are the Lord's instructions: "My word was given the shepherds; they did not receive. *You will not enter into further discussion*." I call Elna that evening and learn she has gotten basically the same word! With her, however, the Lord used the word "dialogue," instead of discussion.

You would think the shepherds would have either received the word that was given them or simply dropped the whole thing and gone on. But not so! This spiritual saga has only just begun. The Lord shows me the devil is about to do all in his power to get us to enter into further discussion, thereby bringing entanglement. Again, I am shown *we must stand fast!*

Following the Lord's instruction, I am led to Nehemiah 6, which I share with Eldrin. This chapter gives the account of how the enemy attempts in many ways to get Nehemiah off the wall, where he is building for the Lord, down into the plain of Ono (the valley of discussion!) to put a stop to the work of God. While this word is burning in my spirit, Eldrin calls from work one day where he "happens" to have the radio on. He tells me to tune in to *Back to the Bible*. The message is on Nehemiah Chapter 6. How can one fully describe God's beautiful confirmation!

There is another interesting sidelight having to do with dialogue. During the Lutheran Charismatic Renewal, a little magazine was published by and for Lutheran Charismatics or anyone else who might benefit. It contained testimonies to the power of God as well as other fine articles. But then, the editor began to enter into "dialogue" with those of position in the traditional Lutheran Church. Much of the magazine was taken up with this so-called dialogue, which I knew was not of God, but rather a device of the enemy to bring this work of the Kingdom through this publication, to naught. "Lord, help us to be wise as serpents and harmless as doves!"

Through Elna it was also learned that elder Mistik had called during the day demanding names of people who had been offended. Gary and Elna declined saying the Lord has shown them their part is over – that it is time for the shepherds to tend their flocks and that there will be no more dialogue. Elder Mistik then tells them there *is* demon possession in the church, but that it is not Elder Eel, but rather Elna and Gary!

Elna tells me she and Gary have been shown by the Lord that they will suffer martyrdom – but that it will be the gift of martyrdom. She already has tremendous peace and joy, she tells me. The Lord has shown them, she says, that they will be excommunicated from the church! But, at that time, she says, the Lord has shown them, the sheep's eyes will be opened; there will be outcries and God's hand of judgment will come down on the leadership. This is all so awesome! My heart goes out to these brave saints. At this point, I am not sure where I fit in but, most assuredly, I will be fasting and praying with all diligence for them.

We learn that Elder Mistik has already called Ricky asking for names of those offended by Elder Eel. Ricky gives two names. I do not feel right in my spirit about this, but again must trust the Lord. It seems the attempt at entanglement has gotten a good start! For some reason, we are not called.

We are still on the mailing list of Bellevue Assembly of God and through a flier received on July 13 comes this word in huge letters: "We can't win the world for Christ, if we lose each other." Oh, how it bore witness with my spirit! We had often talked of Golgotha and that if all, who came had stayed, there would be a thousand members. A word of caution, however, numbers do not necessarily mean a move of God or the presence of the Holy Spirit.

It is now Friday, July 15. Eldrin calls Ricky and asks him to usher tomorrow evening for the CBN Premiere with which Full Gospel is involved. Ricky tells him Gary and Elna are being called into Pastor Birdsong's office tomorrow at 1:00!

The next morning at 9:00 Pastor Birdsong calls inviting us to be present at the meeting at 1:00 wherein they will counsel Gary and Elna. Later, Elna calls to ask if we are coming in. I ask her what they want us to do and if they want us there. She said it was up to us – that the Lord had already prepared them and shown them they would be going before the accusers. I do not understand. Did not the Lord say, "no more dialogue?"

Shortly after 1:00, Eldrin, Janet and I join hands and pray for Gary and Elna. Just as we finish praying, the phone rings. It's Pastor Birdsong asking why we are not there! He begins to make demands – says it is obvious we are not submitting to leadership, tells Eldrin we are no longer under Golgotha's "covering" and that we will no longer minister to, or counsel with, anyone at Golgotha. The conversation finally gets so out of hand that Eldrin hangs up. I have been fasting and praying but at that point I leave my family to get alone with the Lord and pray.

At 2:30, Elder Mistik calls – tells Eldrin they (the leadership) need to come right out. Eldrin tells him we have plans and Elder Mistik wants to know what they are. Eldrin tells him he is in charge of ushering for the CBN Premiere and must be there early. Then Elder Mistik tells Eldrin they will be out tomorrow after church. Again, Eldrin tells him we have other plans – guests coming from home. Elder Mistik is persistent and Eldrin tells him if they come they will not be welcome – that this is our home.

Elder Mistik then says he doesn't want us getting information "second-hand" from Gary and Elna. He tells Eldrin we are no longer under the "covering" of Golgotha and that we will no longer minister to anyone there. Eldrin tells him that we have not gone to anyone to minister or counsel – that they had always come to us. Eldrin tells Elder Mistik they have not heard the word that was given the shepherds. This conversation, also, gets so out of hand that Eldrin (to break it off) tells Elder Mistik that he will call him back.

Another word comes on July 16 – this one brought Psalm 121 on a postcard from Arnie vacationing in Colorado. This beautiful Psalm speaks three times of God's keeping power. How I need and will continue to need this blessed assurance! Twice more on separate occasions in time to come, this Psalm will be given through Ariel.

On Monday, July 18, I call Elna to ask about Saturday. She said she was under fire for one and a half hours, was accused of being rebellious, unsubmissive, and of having an unrepentant heart. They tell her these are the first steps before excommunication. Elna said the power of the enemy was so strong that she almost went under and confessed to all they were accusing her of! Finally, Gary, seeing that things were getting to be too much for Elna, ended the meeting by saying he has to go to work. The duress was so great that Elna said the Lord was taking them off the front lines to be away for two weeks on R&R (rest and recreation).

She said she called Pastor Birdsong to tell him they would be away to rest for two weeks and would not be at church and she said Pastor Birdsong "seemed to understand..." She also said she knew they would have to go to Pastor Birdsong and Elder Mistik (who were in charge of the "counseling session") to ask forgiveness...I am feeling more and more uncomfortable. *This is entanglement*!

Ricky calls that evening, tells Eldrin that Pastor Birdsong had called Saturday night and told him he was going to announce publicly in church the next morning that Chris and Eldrin Linneman were no longer to counsel with or minister to anyone at Golgotha. Ricky said he was so bothered by this he didn't sleep all night. The next morning at church, he told Elder Mistik that if they announced this, it would be a big mistake and that they would be very sorry. We were there and knew, of course, that it had not been announced, yet, I know by the Spirit of God, that for us there will be no rest and recreation. We will remain on the front lines where, with all our hearts, we must watch and pray, looking to Jesus, our Shepherd, to keep us from being ensnared by the wolves who are closing in.

Chapter Fifteen

THE TRIBUNAL

"But beware of men; for they will deliver you up to the councils, and they will scourge you in their synagogues."
(Matthew 10:17)

On Sunday, July 24, a word greatly blesses me from the cover of the church bulletin: *"Mary...sat at the Lord's feet and listened to His teaching"* (Luke 10:39, RSV). After I was baptized in the Spirit, I had written my parents and told them that I felt as Mary who sat at Jesus' feet (twice, in time to come, a similar word will be given me in prophetic fashion). Now, seven years later, I still feel the same way. I just want to sit at Jesus' feet, to hear His voice, to love and worship Him *and to obey Him.* I find myself "praying without ceasing" and often, for two to three hour sessions, day or night, I'm in my prayer closet seeking the Lord during this critical time. I *must* stay on track. I *must* draw strength from Him.

Our phone rings incessantly that week. We are not answering. We know it is leadership and finally take the phone off the hook. The following Sunday, July 31, we are met by leadership in the foyer of the church as we attempt to leave. Once again, they tell us we are un-submissive to church leadership, that we are under church discipline and that, if we do not have a change of heart and come before leadership, the charges against us will be read publicly before the congregation. We are also told we have been barred from taking the Lord's Supper. Once again, I tell these leaders – Pastor Birdsong, Elder Mistik and Elder Thair – that God's word was given the shepherds, that they did not receive and that we are *not* to enter into further discussion. Pastor Birdsong tells me this is a "false word" whereupon Eldrin takes my arm and escorts us out of the church.

That afternoon, Mitch calls. They are now in that spiritual "hothouse," Christ the King Church, in San Angelo, Texas. He shares that not only has he been water baptized via immersion, but he and Mary also have been baptized in the Holy Spirit. Glory to God! We've shared with them what has been going on at Golgotha and they have had us much on their minds. Their church is praying for us. What a blessing! The Lord's timing is perfect and beautiful!

The next day, Monday August 1st, I experience some of the heaviest warfare I have ever known. It occurs through the night and the next morning I vividly recall getting the word, "tribunal," during that time of fitful sleep. I tell Eldrin I'm sure I've gotten another word from the Lord. I know that Jesus went before the Tribunal and I look up the word to find, "a court of justice." The Lord directs me to the word "tribune" that follows and I find these meanings: "In ancient Rome, an official or magistrate, especially one whose duty was to protect citizens of the common class from unfair treatment by magistrates of the noble class" and "any defender of the people" ...WOW! What powerful confirmation as to where the Lord has placed me! And now, He is disclosing that we will, indeed, be going before the tribunal.

I call Elna and share what the Lord has given me. To my amazement, she says that just that morning she had told Bonnie, a Christian friend and co-worker, that they (she and Gary) would be going before the tribunal tonight! Once again, they have been called in to go before the leadership. My heart, by now, has grown heavy. I know that Elna and Gary can no longer be trusted. They have fallen under the controlling power of the devil operating through leadership and have disobeyed God by entering into much dialogue.

By Wednesday, August 3, my spirit is very heavy. I know that we are alone and that our time is very near. The Lord now gives liberty to call Geri. It will be our first telephone conversation. Our contacts at Golgotha have been brief, powerful, God-ordained. I know the importance of allowing the Lord to arrange my contacts and this contact, also, will be wholly God ordained, powerful, full of confirmation.

"Geri," I say after identifying myself, "we may be excommunicated from the church!" From the other end of the line comes a glorious, "HALLELUJAH!!!" That alone, is enough to bring confirmation, encouragement and a mighty charge to my spirit. From notes made before the call, I now share everything with Geri – from the word having to do with my calling, to the word about the hierarchy, to the word given the shepherds, etc. I mention how those raised up to go with us (now also including Ricky), seem to have fallen completely under the manipulative power of the leadership and that, from all appearances, Eldrin and I are in this thing alone. I mention the accusations that have been brought against us and, Geri, already familiar with the devil's tactics along this line, says, "I can't believe it; the devil is still using the same old words!"

By the spirit, Geri already knows, basically, everything that has been taking place. "This thing," she says, "is going to uproot itself." She confirms everything that I have felt by the Spirit to do or not to do. Just that morning she said she had had a heavy burden for me and went into travail until it lifted. Also, she said she had been invited to some special function that day that she really wanted to attend, but the Lord kept her home. She now knows the reason why. Geri assures me that I am right on track and that I must stand fast and listen only to the Holy Spirit.

That evening, Elna calls to report on Monday's meeting with the leadership. There is an immediate check in my spirit. Elna says the leadership was hostile at first, but then completely changed and there was "reconciliation." I told her this seemed great but how could they accuse her of demon possession, rebellion, an unsubmissive spirit and an unrepentant heart and then do a complete about-face? I also asked her about the word God had given her "no more dialogue, you (Elna and Gary) will be martyred, you (Elna and Gary) will be excommunicated and then the sheep's eyes will be opened, etc." She seemed not to hear and then starts bringing accusations against me! She tells me I need to go to the leadership and "seek reconciliation." The power of the enemy working through Elna is so great that I literally feel sick.

Somehow, I get off the phone. My spirit is so exceedingly heavy that I can hardly speak. I step out onto the front porch and walk up and down the walkway unable to talk or pray, but simply agonizing before the Lord. It is a taste of dark Gethsemane. Eldrin follows me out and sits quietly on the porch knowing he can say or do nothing to ease this cup of suffering. I am not sure how long we are there but, finally, Eldrin says, "Chris, I don't know how you feel, but I think you should call Geri back."

Once again, there is that "green light." I share with Geri Elna's call. She wants to know how long I have known Elna and says Satan is really working through her. She says all that dialogue and discussion are from the pit and that we need to watch out when someone tells us we ought to do this or that. Again, Geri exhorts me to stand fast and to listen only to the Holy Spirit; "He will not lead you astray."

On Thursday, August 4, there is an attempt by the postman to deliver a certified letter to our door. Several days before, the Lord had spoken to Eldrin, "Golgotha's leadership will try to deliver a certified letter. *Don't sign for it!"* So, when the doorbell rings, I know it is that certified letter ordering us to come before leadership and I do not answer the door. Later, we get the pink slip "attempt to deliver," in our mailbox.

At times, because of the gravity of the situation, Eldrin and I would just look at one another and I would say, "If this thing were not so deadly serious, it would be hilariously funny." Then, we would start to laugh and we would laugh and laugh from deep within. We knew that the joy of the Lord was our strength (Nehemiah 8:10) and we also knew that this was Holy Ghost laughter that brought a blessed release.

The next day, Friday, August 5, the inner knowing that this "thing" is about to come to a head, plus the fire and zeal of the Lord burning within are such that I can hardly contain myself. I write out this prayer before the Lord – "My prayers which the Lord has laid on my heart concerning the leadership of Golgotha" – '*And, now, Lord, behold their threatenings: and grant unto thy servants, that with all boldness, they may speak thy word*' (Acts 4:29). I also pray, "Lord, if there is to be anyone else with us (Eldrin and I) in this in one accord have them call tonight and let Eldrin answer." No one calls.

The flesh still trembles at what is ahead and the Lord reminds me of a little saying He had given me for Janet when she was going through a particularly difficult time in high school. It simply said, "When the going gets tough, the tough get going!" It was not Scripture, as such, but I knew it was a word from the Lord for her. I had written it out in large letters on a sheet of yellow paper. The Lord now instructs me to get out that sheet of yellow paper, which had been saved, and place it on the counter next to the kitchen stove. There, it will constantly remind me of His power within.

That evening, August 5, Don, from Golgotha, pays us a visit. He has an "in" with the leadership and has been talking to them. He feels the Lord has called him to be a mediator and comes to try to convince us we must be "reconciled." Patiently, we again go over everything telling him that, via God's instructions, we are not to enter into further discussion. Reluctantly, with disappointment, he finally leaves.

On Saturday, August 6, a couple from Golgotha appears at our door. They have been going through a very difficult time and the "counsel" of the leadership has left them all but devastated. Threats of excommunication have been leveled against them. I can pray and lend a compassionate ear, but I am very certain that, above all, the Lord has sent them as just one more confirmation of what is taking place in Golgotha's "inner sanctum" and that nothing has changed as Elna had reported.

That evening, August 6, Don returns. This time he has a letter from Golgotha's leadership. It contains the principles of Matthew 18 used for excommunication. We do not receive the letter, nor do we even look at it. Once again, Don tries to convince us to talk with leadership and to be "reconciled." Once again, we tell him we must continue to stand on what the Lord has told us to do and that there is to be no more discussion.

Don then begins to express his own heart. He says that he was in no way satisfied with the way things were handled with a close loved one and Elder Eel, and that he plans to get to the "bottom of it" when Elder Eel returns from out of state. He also says there is no love in the leadership and that they give that "great father image of being up on a throne." Then Don tells us that Pastor Birdsong and the elders "are very afraid of this situation (our excommunication) dividing the congregation." Inside, I almost want to laugh. I can only think, "Who are we that our expulsion would divide the congregation? ...unless God is in it."

Then Don goes on to say that Christ wants reconciliation and that He does not want His church to divide. Without forethought, under God's anointing, out of my mouth comes these words: "Look Don, before it's all over, the Lord is going to divide and divide and divide and purify, until He's got a people entirely His own filled with His power and boldness to get His work done before He returns." Don seems to understand and says, "I want to be among them." He then says, "You realize they plan to excommunicate you and will make the announcement at church tomorrow." We said we knew. I tell Don I had just finished reading the Bible again, via my daily Bible reading plan, and had asked the Lord where he now wanted me to go. The Lord led me straight to the Gospels, I told Don, to take a long, hard look at the trial and crucifixion of Jesus. I said I did not want to see it, but had known for some time that we would be "crucified" at Golgotha. Don just shook his head and said he didn't think he would have that kind of strength.

Again, on this second visit, Don shows a true Christian spirit along with genuine love and concern for us. Once again, he tells us how much he appreciated the contact with us when he first came to Full Gospel. He tells us he loves us as a brother and sister in the Lord, gives us a hug and leaves.

Although the Lord had prepared us, there is no way to fully describe the next morning, Sunday, August 7, 1983, when an entire sermon is preached against "a couple" in the congregation. We, of course, know that the couple is us. At the end of the message, our names are mentioned along with the plans for excommunication. The Holy Spirit had exhorted me continually to walk upright before God and man and later we learned that people had no idea of who was being preached against and asked of themselves, "Is it I?"

The Scripture lesson and message for that Sunday is taken from Micah 6:1-8. The most difficult accusation to bear is this word (in essence) which is directly against us: "The Lord has a controversy (case) against you and has come down out of His heaven to take up the matter...Be quick to repent!"

Hebrews 4:12 says that "*the word of God is quick, and powerful, and sharper than any two-edged sword.*" It has been said if that word is used against us wrongly, it can cut us to pieces and leave us bleeding to death in the ditch. I know this is true. As one accusation after another is hurled against us, Eldrin says over and over, "Chris, don't receive it. Chris, don't receive it!!" With my head bowed low before the Lord, I pray in tongues the entire time. All through the service I am enabled to praise the Lord for allowing me to share in His sufferings and to meditate on two Scriptures the Holy Spirit brings before me continually - "*The Lord is my Shepherd; I shall not want*" (Psalm 23:1) and "*We must obey God rather than men*" (Acts 5:29, RSV).

At the close of the service, Pastor Birdsong announces that the Scripture lesson and message had been very pointed and intentionally so "because they were pointed at a couple in the congregation – Eldrin and Chris Linneman – who will not communicate or seek reconciliation, because they say they've gotten a word from God."

Later, we are able, somehow, to acquire a tape, but, at a point in time when I feel I have the strength to again listen to the message, it will not play! It is so faint it cannot be heard! I felt the Lord say, "I will not allow you to be subjected again to this message."

The Lord's Supper is served that Sunday. Before the invitation is given to come forward, it is announced that those who have "ought" against anyone are not to participate. We know this means us. After this announcement is made, Pastor Birdsong and our elder come back to where we are seated. They want to know if we will be "reconciled." Eldrin shakes his head, "no," and then Pastor Birdsong turns to me and asks if I feel the same way. I nod, "yes." Later, I think, "what they really meant was will you compromise with the devil?!"

By this time, precious sister Glenda, has made her way back to where we are seated. Glenda and I have had several God-appointed encounters. God has given her discernment. She takes the seat next to me and gives me a hug. She is crying and obviously very vexed. I tell her the Lord has shown us we will be going through "crucifixion." She starts to weep profusely and with strong emotion – as though she had not heard a word I said – tells me, *"Chris, they are going to crucify you!"* Once again, I tell her that I know and that it is all right - that the Lord has prepared us. *The Lord uses me to comfort Glenda.*

After the service, precious little Terri, Geri's daughter, comes to me with warmth and love, gives me a hug and slips a tape into my hands that her mother said to give me (it's a tape exposing shepherdship!). Terri tells me to call should I need prayer or just to share. Terri and her husband have been faithful members of Golgotha, yet I've noticed their attendance has become less and less regular. As with Glenda, I know the Lord has them here this morning just for me.

By God's grace, we've made it through perhaps the most difficult time we will ever face. Yet, it is not over...there will be a waiting period – how long we do not know. We only know we must stay at Golgotha and face the devil head-on until final excommunication papers are served...or however they do it.

In the meantime, the Holy Spirit reminds me that, like Jesus, we have gone before the "tribunal" to face a mock "trial" where we were falsely accused and sentenced to "death" at Golgotha.

Chapter Sixteen

THE VIA DOLOROSA
(The "Sorrowful Way")

"He is despised and rejected of men; a man of sorrows,
and acquainted with grief."   *(Isaiah 53:3)*

After completing the previous chapter, I continue with "The Crucifixion," which I think will be the next chapter title. But the chapter grows to such length that it needs to be divided. This puts me in a quandary for a new chapter title. Turning to the Lord, I am immediately given "The Via Dolorosa." I know it means "the road of sorrows," or something similar, but I want to be accurate so I begin what I feel might be a long diligent search. Picking up one of my Bible dictionaries with the intention of turning to the "V" section, I open instead to the last page, which contains a black and white photo. Up from the bottom of the page comes this caption: "along the via Dolorosa ('the sorrowful way') in Jerusalem"! Quietly, I weep before the Lord realizing once again the very real presence and direction of the Holy Spirit as He quickly supplies and confirms a new chapter title.

You may be thinking we have no right to compare ourselves to the Lord as He walked that sorrowful way from Pilate's judgment seat to His crucifixion. Yet we, too, as we follow in obedience to Jesus (refusing to bow to man), will certainly know something of that way of sorrows. Just as Jesus was indicted, now we, too, must set our face "like a flint" to follow Jesus all the way from the courtroom to our own "crucifixion."

By God's grace, we've lived through "the sermon" and now night has come. After finally getting to sleep, I am awakened at 3:00 am. (Monday, August 8, 1983) with these words: "Jesus Christ *is* truth; He loves truth." How simple and profound! I get up and jot down these words along with other thoughts I feel the Lord is giving me. Will I be allowed to speak before the congregation? In my spirit I know differently, yet, "just in case," I write *this "open letter" to the church:*

"Jesus Christ is Truth; He loves truth. yet there has been such a perversion of that truth by leadership since we first confronted them almost a month ago, that hardly any semblance of that truth remains. My family is battle-weary, yet our spirits are strong in that stand God has called us to take at Golgotha.

At least two years ago, Elder Mistik whom I loved and respected — because at that time I sensed the anointing of God upon him, told me — and I quote "Chris, you seem to have an almost prophetic calling, yet I sense a fear in you. The day is coming when you are going to have to speak out in boldness but then leave whatever you say on the altar.

*Not only can this prophetic calling be keenly sensed throughout my book, **There's More to be Had,** but it has been confirmed again and again in the past seven years with the most recent confirmation coming last November and December, through two anointed women of God. Had I been given a choice, I would have chosen a different calling, yet, God's gifts and calling are without repentance and by His grace, I will walk in that calling for which He has chosen me.*

My only desire has been to go for the Lord, to speak for the Lord, to break down the devil's strongholds and to free the sheep who have been bitten and devoured by the enemy. Although the leadership has made every attempt through harassment, manipulation and threats to make us take back the Word from the altar, that word remains."

That evening, two sisters from Golgotha pay me a visit. The Holy Spirit gives alert. They stay from 7:00 till almost 1:00 the next morning. They talk of "the sermon" and how wrong it was. One dear sister is confused. The other is again used by the enemy that evening. In spite of the fact that she knows she was strongly used by the devil most recently to try to knock me off course, there are no apologies, no signs of remorse. I ask her forgiveness for any thoughts I may have had against her. Among other things, she says she feels the Lord has "exonerated" her to speak to leadership on my behalf – to ask them to allow me to speak to the congregation. I recall the "open letter" written early that morning yet something doesn't fit...something isn't right. I must continue to wait very carefully on the Lord no matter who comes telling me this or that.

Along the way, there has been temptation to gather around us those who might be "like-minded," but over and over I hear the Lord's final instructions – *"Trust no man"* (from Jeremiah 17:5, my emphasis). The Lord lets me know that in no way am I to defend myself and that He, Himself, will be my defense. What a blessed promise; still, the way is not easy. By now, the most difficult aspect of this whole scenario is to be misunderstood. We want people to understand us and we want to be vindicated in their eyes. But, for me, the opportunity to "clear" myself will never come and I will never again hear from the one who felt she was exonerated to speak on my behalf.

On Wednesday, August 10, a note comes in the mail from Sandy. She says she doesn't understand the circumstances at Golgotha, but, as she was praying, she felt certain Scriptures were for me. Janet is at home at the time and knows I can use some encouragement. She grabs my Bible and starts to read. All of the Scriptures apply in a beautiful way, but as she reads the second one listed, I literally go into spiritual orbit. Genesis 50:20 says, "As for you, ye thought evil against me; but God meant it unto good, to bring to pass, as it is this day, to *save much people alive*" (my emphasis).

These are Joseph's words to his brothers who had sold him into slavery years earlier. Ultimately, Joseph becomes second in command in Egypt where God uses him to save not only his brothers from destruction, but the people of Israel as well. The confirmation that comes through this Scripture is among the most powerful I have received. The Lord has shown me repeatedly and, now, through this word that, like Joseph, He has placed me in the Body of Christ as a protector and a deliverer.

From Genesis 50:20, there is a reference in my Bible to Psalms 56:5 which says, "*Every day they wrest* [twist] *my words; all their thoughts are against me for evil.*" This is simply confirmation of what we had known all along and of what had been written in my open letter.

That afternoon, as I am praying in the spirit, the Lord puts Psalm 91 strongly on my heart leading me to the following verse: "*He shall cover thee with His feathers, and under His wings shalt thou trust: His truth shall be thy shield and buckler*" *(verse 4, my emphasis).* The last half of the verse is especially quickened as a word from the Lord. Here is that word *truth* again! When I realize how this ties in with the word the Lord awakened me with early Monday morning – "Jesus Christ *is* Truth; He loves truth" – I get really excited. How beautifully the Lord continues to tie it all together with his blessed confirmation!

That afternoon (Wednesday, August 10) a brother from Golgotha comes to call. There is a check in my spirit and I wonder about his motives. Once again, I find myself sharing what God has called me to do. He, too, feels he has favor with Pastor Birdsong and thinks that Cover Church should be involved. I am beginning to understand the check. We feel he was sent by Golgotha's leadership and I make it plain *we will continue to stand* in what God has called us to do regardless of the pressure or the power.

It is Sunday, August 14. It has been a week since that infamous sermon was preached and, according to God's orders, we head back to Golgotha. We pray that the Lord will enable us to walk wholly in His love and wisdom. Once again the cover of the church bulletin contains a word in due season. It pictures a time clock and simply says, "Be Ready..."

The sermon that morning goes back to the old "status quo" except that much effort is made to bring life and joy into the place both through the sermon and through the music ministry. No mention is made of us or of last Sunday's sermon. Again, I pray throughout the entire service sensing extreme heaviness especially when a certain elder gets up to present the Scripture readings.

Several people come to us after the service. Most show genuine love and concern, and all, in one way or another, are under confusion. Iris comes whom the Lord had used a couple times in my life in a beautiful way. She says she doesn't understand what is going on, but loves us and is praying for us. She says she had gone to leadership last Sunday to find out what was going on, but all she got was "double-talk" and "could not get the straight of anything."

Precious Jimmy and Glenda come. Glenda looks as though she hasn't slept all week and Jimmy seems very distressed and even angry in his spirit over recent events. I tell them to read Psalm 56, which the Lord has given me – especially, the first six verses and, specifically, verse 5 in order to know what has been going on (*"Every day they wrest* [twist] *my words: all their thoughts are against me for evil,"* Psalm 56:5).

Our elder's wife shows genuine love and concern – says she is so glad to see us there. She seems really surprised that after last Sunday's sermon we came back. I tell her of the holy fire of the past seven years that has prepared us and brought us to this place and how the Lord has told us to stand fast. I tell her of the office and prophetic calling God has placed on my life. In her eyes and spirit I can see she perceives and understands. She tells me, "If we can stand fast through this fire, we are all going to be purified."

It is now Wednesday, August 17. It is between 8:30 and 9:00 in the evening and I am still outside watering flowers when I see headlights turn into our lane. The Holy Spirit lets me know it is leadership and I race to get into the house and up to my prayer closet to pray. Eldrin comes up a short time later to let me know it is our elder and Elder Mistik. Later, Eldrin tells me it was extremely awkward before I came down and gave each a hug and served lemonade. It was the beginning of an evening that lasted until 1:30 a.m.

It is important now to clarify a point. Our elder and Elder Eel had not been present for our July 12th meeting with leadership and I now know that this evening has been ordained of God for our elder to hear first-hand what the Lord has given me. I know, too, that the Lord has paved the way to even let these two into the house through our elder's wife who had shown love and concern for us on Sunday.

Once more, I find myself going through everything the Lord has given me – from the words having to do with my position and calling, to the word having to do with the hierarchy, to the most recent word given the shepherds, "feed my sheep" and Jeremiah 23:1-4. Our elder takes many notes. Apparently, he has not heard what the Lord has given me from anyone else or if he has, it has been in a distorted fashion.

Elder Mistik again takes notes even though he has previously heard everything. As I share, he attempts to twist everything I say, but the Lord holds me fast and even our elder would stop Elder Mistik and say, "That is not what I'm hearing her say." Had our elder not been present, the whole evening would have been disastrous, but the Lord would not have allowed us to talk to Elder Mistik alone.

From notes written later, I wrote, "I really believe Elder Mistik has become the devil's henchman to implement this ungodly shepherdship to the hilt." He strongly emphasized that he planned to bring in the "under-shepherds," in addition to the shepherds (pastors and elders, etc.) to keep everything under control.

Elder Mistik asks me how I know I am hearing from God and then tells me at least two or three times to "be careful" – that "there are a lot of false prophets running around." At times he stares at me and it is like a gaze from the pit of hell...

Before they leave, I am reminded of a vision recently given one of the members. Arnie had heard it first-hand on his way out of town Friday, August 12, and came out with much excitement to share. In this vision, there is a courtroom with the people of Golgotha in a cage bound, blindfolded and gagged. People with staffs (shepherds) are also seen as well as people with scrolls (teachers). They are all in bondage. They have forgotten their First Love. The Father God can be seen on His throne. There is a sword pulled part way out of its sheath containing Scriptures that at first cannot be seen. Later, these Scriptures clear to the viewer and Jeremiah 23:1-4 can be seen on the sword!

I ask our elder and Elder Mistik if they have heard this vision. They look at each other and then say, "yes." It was quite apparent they never intended to share this vision. I again remind them of the word "tribunal" and "tribune" the Lord had given me about two weeks after Jeremiah 23:1-4 was given the leadership and less than a week before the sermon was preached against us (our trial and indictment). I ask them how much more evidence they need! Again, I emphasize how tribunal means "courtroom" and tribune has to do with defending the people, or sheep, which ties in with "toe" having to do with balance, circulation and well being of the entire body and "conduit" with it's second meaning, "protector." I also mention again how the Lord has shown me I am a "watchman (prophet) unto the house of the Lord."

By this time Elder Mistik has become indignant and says to me quite loudly, "Chris, you don't have to defend the sheep, Jesus defends the sheep!" I simply say, *"Yes, but he uses people."* In spite of all I have seen and have known in the Spirit to this point, I'm still aghast, hardly able to believe how Elder Mistik tried to twist everything I've said this evening.

In conclusion, Elder Mistik says, "We are going to pray over what you have given us but, then, what are you going to do if none of this is received?" We say nothing knowing for a certainty what the Lord has already shown us. Elder Mistik again says, "How do you know you hear from God?" Again, we are silent. There is no need for further discussion with this man. Indeed, God has forbidden it. He then says, "Well, what if I thought the Lord spoke to me and said, 'take a bulldozer and destroy all of Golgotha and start over?'" Little did he know that, in time, the Lord would do that very thing – not with a bulldozer, but by His Spirit.

The Lord has disclosed what is ahead for us but at this point we have not been shown the final outcome of a church called Golgotha. It has been over a month since we confronted leadership with the Word of the Lord. "How much longer, Lord?" we wonder. We get no specific answer but know by the Spirit our excommuni-cation cannot be far off. In the meantime we continue to follow as Jesus leads our own footsteps along the Via Dolorosa.

On my refrigerator, for many years, has hung a poem that has touched me deeply. Dear reader, if you have read thus far, you too, are surely committed to following Jesus all the way. The poem must be included here:

~The Followers~
They followed him by
thousands
When he served them fish
and bread
And a banquet in the
desert
By His miracle was
spread.
They sang a loud
"Hosanna!"
And they shouted,
"Praise His name"
When in an hour of glory
To Jerusalem He came.
They followed when He
told them
Of a kingdom and a
throne.
But when He went to
Calvary,
He went there all alone.

It seems that many people
Still would follow him
today

If he only went to places
Where everything was
play.
For the kingdom that
they're seeking
Isn't one that's made of
thorns.
They would rather march
in splendor
Mid the blare of drums
and horns.
Oh, they'll follow for the
fishes
Over land and over sea.
And they'll join the
church at Zion,
But not at Calvary.

It's so easy friends to
follow
When the nets are full of
fish,
When the loaves are
spread before you,
And you're eating all you
wish.
When no lands, nor lots,
nor houses,
And no friendships are at
stake,
When there's no mob to
mock you
And you have no cross to
take.
But you'll need some
faith to follow,
Down through
Gethsemane.

And you'll need some
love to follow Him
Right up to Calvary.
~Selected~

Chapter Seventeen

THE CRUCIFIXION

"Yea, the time cometh, that whosoever killeth you will think that he doeth God service."   *(John 16:2)*

It is now Sunday, August 21. Sandy comes before the service with Psalm 69, which she feels is a Word from the Lord for me. How familiar I am especially with this verse: *"For the zeal of thine house hath eaten me up; and the reproaches of them that reproached thee are fallen upon me"* (Psalm 69:9). Quickened to my spirit as a Word from the Lord shortly after the Baptism, it was again brought back strongly before the July 12 meeting with the leadership. Now, here it is again!

This morning's message is on (of all things) faith! Once again, I know it is only a token dangled before the people – a "pacifier" for the present and that nothing has changed. Before the sermon, Elder Thair reads and comments on the Scriptures listed on the back of the bulletin and then quotes from the writings of Watchman Nee...

It is necessary now to comment on the works of Watchman Nee, an early Christian author of Chinese origin whose writings are deep and heavily into spiritual authority. At one point, one of Nee's books came into my possession but, beyond one chapter, I had no leading to read it.

Later, when the Lord instructed me to call Geri, I shared at the end of our conversation how Arnie, the young man who had lived with us, had left Golgotha and was now attending a campus fellowship named Maranatha. There was silence on the other end of the line and then Geri told me that Maranatha, also, was heavily under (ungodly) shepherdship with its focus strongly on the teachings of Watchman Nee! I knew I had to pass this information on to Arnie who stood at first in shock and unbelief, but later literally fled that place because of the tightening noose of manipulation and control.

It's apparent by now that, not only has Golgotha's leadership been into the teachings of Watchman Nee, but at the back of the church hangs a plaque that contains a writing by one of "the Ft. Lauderdale Five." These five men, called out and anointed of God, were eventually used to release the concepts of ungodly shepherdship in every direction.

Back to the Sunday at hand – August 21, 1983. As we are leaving, Elder Eel is waiting at the back door. He reaches out to give me a hug. Always stoic, he has not made any attempt during the past seven years, to reach out in any way. He says we need to get together. I am repulsed feeling unclean in the presence of this man and tell him we will wait on the Lord. He smiles that placid smile and tells me he is ready at any time...Once again, I am sure I see a gaze that emanates from the pit of hell.

That evening, we are away but Arnie stops by and leaves a note containing the following Scripture: "The beast of the field shall honor me, the dragons and the owls; *because I give waters in the wilderness, and rivers in the desert, to give drink to my people"* (Isaiah 43:20, my emphasis). Arnie says he doesn't know how it applies, but the Scripture came up for us as he prayed. To me, it is a word of encouragement from the Lord – that *He will bring Living Water to His people* despite the sleight of man. The next Sunday is basically uneventful, but the week that follows holds much in the way of prophetic confirmation concerning the day and the hour. This confirmation comes through two letters – one from my dad and the other from a sister in the Lord.

I had written a little note to my dad telling him we are not answering the phone because of harassing phone calls and that we are going through a fiery trial that has to do with the call of God on my life. My dad is old and alone and, beyond this, I do not want to burden him. He writes back saying he feels the trial has to do with our church and gave me the following Scripture:

"Rejoice ye in that day, and leap for joy: for, behold, your reward is great in heaven: for in the like manner did their fathers unto the prophets." (Luke 6:23)

As though this Scripture were not enough, another letter comes on the same day from Shirley who attends another church but knows something of the trial we're going through. She said the Holy Spirit spoke to her in her work place to write me a letter and He would tell her what to say. She went in to the hospital chapel, got the big Bible from its stand and prayed for a word for me. She flipped open the Bible and her eyes fell upon the following Scripture:

"Be strong and of good courage, fear not, nor be afraid of them: for the Lord thy God, He it is that doth go with thee; He will not fail thee, nor forsake thee."
(Deuteronomy 31:6)

Shirley then said that she asked the Lord to give her something else for me. She again flipped open the Bible and it opened to the following section of Scripture:

"And whosoever shall not receive you, nor hear your words, when ye depart out of that house or city, shake off the dust of your feet. Verily I say unto you, it shall be more tolerable for the land of Sodom and Gomorrah in the day of judgment, than for that city. Behold, I send you forth as sheep in the midst of wolves: be ye therefore

wise as serpents, and harmless as doves. But beware of men: for they will deliver you up to the councils, and they will scourge you in their synagogues; and ye shall be brought before governors and kings for my sake, for a testimony against them and the gentiles. But when they deliver you up, take no thought how or what ye shall speak: for it shall be given you in that same hour what ye shall speak: for it is not ye that speak, but the Spirit of your Father which speaketh in you."

(Matthew 10:14-20)

Shirley said the Lord also gave her Psalms 3 and Psalms 35. Both are cries for deliverance from "those who persecute without a cause." She called my attention especially to the following verse:

"But thou, O Lord, art a shield for me; my glory, and the lifter up of mine head."

(Psalms 3:3, my emphasis)

The Scriptures that come through the mail on this day, Wednesday August 31, 1983, so quicken to my spirit that I know they have come straight from the throne room of God. From what I am sensing in the spirit our excommunication cannot be more than days away.

We have come to another Sunday, September 4, and again we are back at Golgotha...waiting. The caption on the front of the bulletin says this: "When you give a feast, invite the poor...and you will be blessed." How my heart continues to ache for the oppressed! The sermon centers on Matthew 7:1-5 which has to do with judging others and how we should not look at the speck in our brother's eye while disregarding the beam in our own. Once again, we know the message is directed straight at us. At one point, these words come from the lips of Pastor Birdsong – "If you reject me, you reject God...!"

During the service, I sit next to Eileen, a precious sister in the Lord. After the Lord's Supper is served, I ask her to pray for us, tell her we have been barred from communion and that this is the third time we've missed. She grabs my hand in love, says they know and are praying for us. She says a lot of things have gone on that they are not happy with. They've had Pastor Birdsong out to their home, she tells me, but got no satisfaction. I share with her some of what the Lord has called me to do and the reason for the persecution. Later, I also share in some detail for the first time with Sandy. I sense now, that the Lord is opening wide the door to share.

On Thursday, September 8, it is necessary to call one of the sisters who had been used as a "spoke" (the devil's instrument). I need to pass along a message from her daughter through my daughter – both away at college. But the "brief" message turns into a lengthy time of sharing in answer to her questions concerning our stand at Golgotha. Whether or not she receives is not important. I only know, by the Spirit of God, she must hear.

It is now Saturday, September 10, 1983. Both Eldrin and I are battling "slough foot." My spirit grows heavier and heavier and then I am sure the Lord is showing me our excommunication will take place *tomorrow*! Eldrin is laying stone just outside the back door on the new home we are completing and I step outside to tell him I feel the Lord is showing me we will face "crucifixion" tomorrow. He reminds me there will be guest ministers from Cover Church at Golgotha tomorrow and that surely Golgotha's leadership would not carry out an excommunication at that time. It seems wholly unreasonable, yet I know what I am sensing in the spirit.

As the evening wears on, this "thing" becomes more and more certain and I start thinking of this one and that one that I must call to ask for prayer. There is something I need first to do upstairs and, as I am going up the steps, the Lord speaks plainly, "You will call no one; I will alert those who are to pray for you."

The next morning, Sunday, September 11, 1983, Terri comes to me as we enter the church. She tells me her mother called early that morning (from out of state) and told Terri to tell me she was praying for me! Praise God for His faithfulness! We take a seat, as usual, near the back of the church. The husband of the sister with whom I had just talked on Thursday sits down in front of us along with their daughter. He turns around, shakes hands with Eldrin, then gets up and takes a seat in our row leaving the seat next to me empty. His wife comes in a short while later and takes that seat. I know it is the Lord.

Shortly before the start of the service, Elder Ire and Elder Eel approach Eldrin. They tell him they will follow through with Matthew 18 this morning. Saying nothing, Eldrin simply nods his head. I am not sure we hear anything of the morning's message. Our trek to the cross is about to end!

During the service, Pastor Birdsong makes an announcement for a time of ministry. The sister in the next seat wants to pray for me and I tell her we need prayer for strength for continued obedience to the Lord in what He has called us to do at Golgotha. Instead, she prays that the fruits be manifest in my life (how long will the devil be able to use other Christians as his chief tools of discouragement and destruction?). My shield of faith is up and the devil's fiery darts are repelled. The sting of persecution is no longer so great. I know our work for the Lord at Golgotha is almost over. "You will need some love to follow Him right up to Calvary," the poem had said!

The service is about to end when this sister says, "You

know, Pastor Birdsong does have concern for this body and he does try to do what's right." I reply, "Yes, but I keep getting from the Lord that there is a double-standard, double-mindedness." She looks at me and says, "Yes." I then share the vision of the courtroom, the words "tribunal" and "tribune" the Lord gave me and how, yesterday, the Lord began to give clear discernment that the leadership had been discussing us and that a decision has been made. I tell her this was confirmed before the service started this morning.

Our conversation is interrupted as Pastor Birdsong makes this announcement, "A meeting will be held immediately following the service concerning the couple who will not receive church discipline. Excommunication procedures will be carried out at that time," The sister next to me looks at me in astonishment. I share the rest of the vision, the sword of the Lord with Scriptures written on it including Jeremiah 23:1-4. She starts to cry saying, "Chris, you are protected, but what about this body – what is going to happen to this leadership?" Has this sister's eyes been opened, I wonder. Has she suddenly gotten revelation from the Lord?

The service is over and we head for the door. There is commotion in the church. Either with my natural eye or with the eye of the spirit (I am not sure which),I see the husband of the couple to whom I had given freely and compassionately of my time (as unto the Lord), and for whom many prayers had gone up. At the front of the church with leadership, he turns on his heels in a quick about-face to acquire the excommunication papers for Pastor Birdsong from the Pastor's office! "Trust no man," the Lord had said...

Several people confront us and, before we can get to the door, we are faced by Pastor Birdsong. "Chris," he says, "you did not get that word from the Lord." Saying nothing I drop my head, unable to look in the eyes of this man I had revered as my pastor. Eldrin takes my arm and pulls me toward the door saying as we go that he keeps getting, "Touch not mine anointed, and do my prophets no harm" (I Chronicles 16:22, Psalms 105:15). I didn't even know that he knew this verse! In the midst of this, the Lord speaks to me, "My word was given the shepherds. They did not receive. I will reduce this place to ashes." I know the Lord means spiritual ashes and that nothing can be sadder. I know, too, that His judgment is fixed. Later this word is confirmed by a member who heard me speak it forth as we left the church.

Many months before, the Lord had spoken, "you will be 'crucified' in this church; I want you to stand fast." And so it has come to pass. With obedience comes great joy in spite of intense trauma and suffering. With our eyes fixed on Jesus, our spirits soar heavenward as we say "goodbye" to a place called Golgotha.

Chapter Eighteen

WATCH AND PRAY!

"Watch and pray that ye enter not into temptation"
(Matthew 26:41)

Golgotha is over, but it is not over. We need rest, but there seems to be no rest. People call or come wanting to know more than they have heard through the leadership and the next morning one of Golgotha's members is at our door. She was brought out by a compassionate sister who found her crying on the church steps because she could not understand why we had been so treated. With her bags, it is obvious she has come to stay.

"Lord," I cry, "if you are in this, *help!* We want to do the right thing." Quickly, we learn that our own lives and privacy are a thing of the past. Nellie is fearful of being alone. She is also an epileptic who, although heavily medicated, is given to grand mal seizures. Her condition took her to the State Mental Institution where she acquired a diploma of which she was quite proud. The epilepsy, however, remained untouched.

Less than a week after Nellie arrives, a grand mal occurs. It is shortly after midnight. We are trying to get some needed sleep when an unearthly scream pierces the silence. "It's Nellie!", I exclaim to Eldrin as I jump to my feet and race for the door. A bright, full moon floods our bedroom. In the hall, I am confronted by stark, raw fear. Only by praying loudly in tongues can I get to Nellie's room.

I am not prepared for the Nellie I see sprawled out on the bed motionless and, apparently, lifeless. The devil speaks,

"Now, lets see what a fine Christian you are! One of Golgotha's members has died in your house!" With pounding heart, I rebuke the devil, pray in tongues and call out to Nellie all at the same time. It seems like forever before Nellie starts to respond, threshing about, sobbing and recounting the horror of the "aura" that surrounded her before the grand mal hit. With my arms around her, I sit on the edge of the bed rocking her back and forth trying to comfort her as a mother would a small child. I listen, pray, tell the devil he will not, in Jesus' name, manifest himself again in such a manner in my house (he doesn't). We are there until the sun comes up. There had been no sleep that night.

It is Sunday morning. I feel we must go to church, but where? Who would want us? We are led to a small country church nearby where the first person to greet us confirms that epilepsy is a spirit. As we leave the church that morning, the Lord lets me know we will be there but for a short time. During the coming weeks, however, the Lord gives me something each week for Nellie which is confirmed, precisely, on the following Sunday. Nellie would look at me and say, "Are you sure they haven't been listening in on our conversation?" Yet, she either will not, nor cannot, receive. She gets down the encyclopedia to "prove" her condition and that the "aura" is real. Recognizing that we are all but depleted, we know other arrangements must be made.

During the time Nellie is with us, the threat is made against Eldrin's life. A persistent suitor – an alcoholic whom Nellie no longer wants to see – becomes irate thinking we are holding Nellie in our home against her will and turning her against him. He calls and she refuses to talk or get together. A counselor by profession at Golgotha is involved and feels he must call to inform us of the danger. Eldrin gets off the phone and we "freeze" with fear. But, then we remember our authority in the Name of Jesus, and bind the spirit of fear in that all-powerful Name. Immediately, we are given peace.

Sometime during the night, we hear gunshots that seems to come from the end of our lane near the mailbox. The next morning, we find our mailbox torn from its stand and on the ground. But praise God, beyond this, there are no further incidents.

Shortly after our excommunication from Golgotha, Pastor Birdsong puts together a two-page typewritten letter of "explanation" which is sent out to the congregation. We, of course, do not receive this letter but Terri brings out a copy along with a three-page, typewritten paper entitled, "Jezebel and the False Prophetesses," written by one of the elders and distributed to the membership. My name is not mentioned but it is apparent, in light of recent happenings, that I am the one targeted with all the evil of the wicked Jezebel.

Through Pastor Birdsong's letter, we learn of the "grounds" for our excommunication. Not once are any of the accusations mentioned that were leveled against us in that Sunday's sermon. Instead, it is stated that we made "slanderous accusations" against Elder Eel accusing him of being "possessed by the devil," or, of being "sold out to the devil." These were Elna's words about which I had had such a check! *I am being falsely accused of Elna's words*! We were also accused of refusing to meet with Elder Eel so that we might be "reconciled"! The Lord had shown me that because these shepherds loved not the truth, He had given them over to a lying spirit (see II Thessalonians 2:10,11 and I Kings 22:23).

Precious Terri is filled with righteous indignation by these latest accusations. With her toddler she had come refusing to leave, until she is sure I am all right. But God's protective mantle is over me and the anointing for what He has called me to do seems stronger than ever. Jesus' words continue to ring in my spirit, *"Rejoice...leap for joy...for in like manner did their fathers unto the prophets"* (Luke 6:23).

By the Spirit of God, I am shown that through our stand for righteousness at Golgotha, the devil's stronghold over leadership has been broken. Indeed, within a short time, a power struggle arises between leadership. They begin to argue among themselves and then head in other directions. A new pastor comes in, but within a relatively short period of time, announces that God has told him to "close the doors." This is confirmed by one of the members and, so, God's prophetic word, "I will reduce this place to ashes," is fulfilled to the letter.

Although we had been so touched and blessed by those who had shown love and concern for us at Golgotha, the time comes when we know we are being shunned. People seem afraid. Perhaps they have been pondering the thought, "How could they possibly stand against church leadership?" We have reason to believe, too, that Golgotha alerted other churches to "beware" of us. Diligently, we seek the Lord for a place to worship where we will be accepted but, as we are visiting a particular church one Sunday, the pastor suddenly stops talking, looks down at us and says, "We know how to deal with people who cause division in the church." And, so our lonely walk begins.

THE DANGERS OF SHEPHERDSHIP

About a year before we left Golgotha, the Lord began to bring confirmation regarding the dark cloud I had sensed in my spirit over Large Church. This church, too, as well as other charismatic churches in the area, have been operating under ungodly shepherdship. Some of the reports that leak out of Large are even more alarming than those that came out of Golgotha. Yet, Large continues to grow in acclaim, and, in time, is featured in a three-page spread in one of the local newspapers. In one picture, the handsome, charismatic pastor is on his knees with face and hands lifted toward heaven.

"Lord!" I cry out once again as I stand in awe of this article, "How can this man be all wrong? He has over 800 members!" Instantly, I hear the Lord's reply, "So did Jim Jones." Jones was the leader of the cult, People's Temple, Jonestown, Guyana, South America where over 900 people followed Jones to their death in a mass murder/suicide pact.

You may be asking if I am comparing churches that practice ungodly shepherdship to a cult. There is much similarity. History unfolds atrocities of the church that are every bit as ugly as those of Jim Jones. While those at Jonestown followed an unrighteous man to their death, millions, throughout history, refusing to bow to man with his rituals and doctrines, have followed the Righteous One, Jesus Christ, to their death.

As I have prayed fervently over this final chapter, the Lord has had me pulling books, or booklets, from our library with such titles as "Damned Through the church," "Born Again Through Infant Baptism?", "The Trail of Blood" (having to do with the millions of Christian martyrs who would not adhere to infant baptism as the means of salvation), "People's Temple, People's Tomb" (an account of Jim Jones and Jonestown, Guyana, South America) and, finally, "Awake, Church!" Each came in their time as confirmation.

The subject of this book is not a light one. It is one about which most are completely naive. Those who have had their eyes opened and have managed to escape the clutches of ungodly shepherdship find themselves running scared. They are the "scattered sheep" of Jeremiah 23 and

Ezekiel 34. Never have these Scriptures been so applicable as they are today. Those who find another church may be more vulnerable than ever before. Wounded and hurting, they are easy prey for a situation that could be even worse than the one they came out of.

Error comes into the church on the back of truth. Truth, when mixed in with half-truth and lies becomes a conglomeration that only the most discerning can see through. At Golgotha, the Lord gave me the analogy of the frog. It is said that a frog thrown into boiling water will jump out immediately, unharmed. But, if placed in cold water before the burner is turned on, will sit right there and boil to death. So it is with shepherdship. Those who visited Golgotha in her latter stages sensed, immediately, that something was wrong. However, those who stay under shepherdship listening to the deception week after week will eventually, like the frog, be deceived – perhaps even unto destruction.

THE VALLEY OF THE SHADOW OF DEATH

It is only by the grace of God that this book, after nineteen years in the writing, is being completed. Because of its nature (exposing religious spirits), the Lord showed me that the devil would try to kill me before its completion.

To confirm this, Eldrin had a dream that left him shaken. In the dream, I was in a pit-like valley, disrobed and on a cross. My body was swollen and burned. In a hut, nearby, demons burned incense to Satan. More demons marched around the foot of the cross chanting "aha, aha! We've got her now! We've got her now!" A barbed wire enclosure kept out would-be rescuers. After repeated attempts, Eldrin got me out of this valley and up into the fresh air and sunshine, where he anointed me with oil and prayed over me until I was healed. This dream had too much spiritual significance to be ignored. I felt it had to do with my health and it was something that, seemingly, could not be broken off.

Then, in late December, 2000, I, too, had a dream. Interestingly, it was just that year, with my son's encouragement and help in reformatting the manuscript, that I had gotten back full swing into writing. In my dream, I was approached by a professionally dressed medical woman wearing a black, veil-like cape. She swung the veil over her face, blew in my face and said, "Receive the spirit of death." This she did three times. Each time, I rebuked her in Jesus' name and she left. But I knew we were up against Goliath.

A short time later, I was diagnosed with full-blown ovarian cancer. Both Eldrin and I already knew by the Spirit of God what medical science had not detected. Our daughter, Janet, a director at one of the local hospitals, gave us precious support and recommended Dr. Patterson, a gynecologic Oncology specialist, who is not only an excellent surgeon, but a fine man and Christian as well.

In the natural, there was one insurmountable problem after another. After surgery, I could not walk. One leg had atrophied and I was given no absolute assurance of ever walking again. As he sat at the foot of my hospital bed and saw that I was unable to walk, Eldrin, who had been standing strong in faith, looked up to heaven and said, "Lord, what's going on here?" In a voice so loud and clear that it shook him, the Lord simply replied. "Trust me." This command held Eldrin like a rock beside me. God's Word came alive to him as never before.

Our son, Mitch, stationed at Canon Air Force Base, new Mexico, also provided invaluable, much needed support. He took leave to be with us and was granted a humanitarian reassignment to be near home. According to medical reports, I had a little over a year to live.

In the eighth month of chemo, I developed an infection that would not go away. During this time, our dreams were fulfilled to the letter. I became both septic and jaundiced. I was given blood transfusions and thirty-five different antibiotics back to back. *Nothing helped.* My body was burned and swollen from the chemo and, twice, my temperature soared to 105 degrees. Janet, "just happened" into the room the first time, noted I didn't "look right," took my temperature and I was quickly placed on the "cooler"! After this, I was monitored even more closely.

Things looked grave. Eldrin called Pastor Dave who announced my situation at church that evening. But before Lenora got back to her seat from the altar, the Lord spoke, *"Go now, to Chris in the hospital room!"* Sharon felt she had gotten the same word. Church was not over, but they left immediately to obey the Lord. Mitch, in my room, joined them in prayer and, later I learned(unknown to me at the time) that my hands were uplifted praising the Lord! When I learned that Lenora and Sharon had been there, the Lord spoke, "I sent them there to set the grim reaper to flight." When I told them, they already knew. They said the spirit of death was all over the room.

The battle was not over. Finally, the bacteriologist told Eldrin, "I've done all I can do. I can't help her." With that, Eldrin said, "I know someone who can" and, in two days, I was out of the hospital and back home.

Where am I now? I'm finishing this book. Hallelujah! "By his stripes I was and am healed" (Isaiah 53:5, I Peter 2:24). "No weapon formed against me shall prosper" (Isaiah 54:17). These Scriptures were written out on small pieces of paper which I taped to my chest before every hospital stay or doctor visit. One doctor asked if I had them there as protection against them. I told him they were there to bolster my own faith.

At least two years before the diagnosis, the Lord had me memorize over forty healing Scriptures that Gloria Copeland used when told she had a fatal disease. The Holy Spirit was preparing ahead of time. From the beginning we stood on healing Scriptures. People would call and Eldrin would tell them God said I was healed. We knew most did not want to hear this but we also knew that my life hung in the balance and that "death and life are in the power of the tongue" (Proverbs 18;21). We will be forever grateful for Rev. Kenneth E. Hagin and others through whose ministries we learned to stand on the authority of God's Word.

AWAKE CHURCH!

Except for the book of Acts and the "great awakenings" of history, the church as we know it has been largely dead or dying not knowing the time on God's clock. But, now, in this final hour, God is surely shaking everything that can be shaken, including the churches. I do not believe there is a denomination that has not been visited in some way by this last outpouring of the Spirit. Yet, sadly, most have refused to accept the Pentecostal power and some (as already noted) have even published documents against it. But nothing will stop this move of God. It will grow in fire and intensity until the Lord takes his people out (See I Thessalonians 4:16,17).

This book is not intended to target charismatic churches, although that is where the devil seems to be operating most feverishly at this time. It only makes sense that, having most churches either dead or asleep, he would descend full-force upon those who have been enlightened by the Spirit to know the truth about salvation, the baptism in the Holy Spirit, the gifts of the Spirit, healing, etc.

When I came into the power of God, the Lord allowed me to sense, in a very powerful way, the demons (religious spirits) that sit over churches – the strongest over the Catholic Church and on down. The hierarchical structure of most churches has turned the church into an organization, rather than the giant, living organism the Lord would have it be, where both fruits and gifts abound (see Galatians 5:22, Romans 12:4-8, I Corinthians 12:8-10, and Ephesians 4:11-16). The five-fold ministry of Ephesians 4:11 – apostles, prophets, evangelists, pastors, and teachers – is set up by God *to equip the saints for ministry* – not to run the show!

During Golgotha, the Lord spoke, "Make detailed notes; you are in a 'hairy' situation." I knew I was in a "hairy" situation, but little did I realize that these notes would later be used for a book! Over and over, as I have written, I have heard the enemy, "There is no need for this book – shepherdship is over." But God has never canceled this assignment. Our experience through the years, as well as the experience of others, and information gleaned from the Internet by my son on "abusive" churches, proves that shepherdship is not only alive and "well," but growing.

The Internet information has simply served to confirm the writings of this book. Again and again, we find such terms as "manipulation and control," "subtle twisting of Scripture," "authoritarianism," "legalism," "deception," "surveillance," "covering," "certain doom if you leave that covering," "undue emphasis on the local church and those tied in with it," "performance and service," "unhealthy dependency upon the church and its leadership and absolute obedience to them," "obsession with discipline," "excommunication," etc. These articles also confirmed what we already know – that many – even intelligent Christians – enjoy being told what to do taking on what is referred to as a "learned helplessness."

One writer states that we must develop "critical discerning minds if we are to avoid the tragedy of churches that abuse." I believe that even more importantly because of the subtlety, we must pray for the gift of the discerning of spirits found in I Corinthians 12:10. The best definition I find of discernment is "keen insight." I have not seen devils, but I have sensed their presence in such a way that I did not have to see them! Discernment is that inner witness that "something just isn't right." When we are given discernment, we must seek God carefully about what to do with it. We must also differentiate between suspicion and discernment. Suspicion is Satan's counterfeit for God's gift of discernment.

We could not end this book without making sure you have the opportunity to get your name written down in the Lamb's book of life (see Revelation 21:27). Don't let religion with all its rituals and doctrines deceive you into hell! Jesus said, "**Ye *must* be born again**" (John 3:7). It is so simple. *Nothing is more important*! Just say this *little prayer:*

> *Dear Lord Jesus,*
>   *I believe that you are the Son of God who died for my sins. I believe you rose from the dead and that you are coming again soon. I ask you to come into my heart right now and cleanse me from all unrighteousness. Baptize me now in your mighty Holy Spirit so I might live for you. Thank you, Lord. Amen.*

After you say this prayer, you can expect a visit from the devil telling you that you have not received anything. Just stand fast. The Word says, *"everyone who asks receives"* (Luke 11:10 RSV). Be sure, now, to confess Jesus before men (see Romans 10:9, 10). If we are ashamed of Him, the Word says He will be ashamed of us before the Father (see Mark 8:38).

Just begin to praise Him now in a precious heavenly language. You must do the speaking. *the Holy Spirit will give the language*! The Bible says in Romans 8:26 that we don't know how to pray as we ought. How true! We need the power promised in Acts 1:8 to witness, to pray, praise, and to overcome.

Ask the Lord to lead you to a loving, Bible-believing church where the Holy Spirit is welcome. There are some good churches and leadership. Praise God for that! There are also home fellowship groups and Christian TV that offer excellent teachings and ministry. The Lord showed me that Christian TV is His giant, end-time harvesting machine. With this too, however, we must exercise discernment.

The Bereans were commended because they searched the Scriptures daily, "*whether those things were so*" (Acts 17:11). They did not swallow everything that came down the "Pike." In addition we are told in I John 4:1 to "*try the spirits whether they are of God.*" Jesus also tells us in Mark 4:24 to "*take heed what ye hear*" and in Galatians 1:6 and II Corinthians 11:4, the Scriptures warn us of "*another gospel*" and "*another Jesus.*" We know it is the spirit of anti-Christ – the spirit of perversion and deception that is blanketing the earth. The religious spirits who put Jesus on the cross are still around and more powerful than ever, because they know their time is short (Revelation 12:12). That is the reason God has commanded this book.

As we understand it, there is even now a large networking of churches brought together, reportedly, to support one another in this hour. While this seems good, other reports have it that this is little more than a giant surveillance system where people from church to church are monitored and checked. How much more organization do we need, how much more surveillance before we have the liberty to be the church of Jesus Christ called by the Master not to make captives, but to set the captives free (Isaiah 61:1, Mark 16:17,18)!

* * * *

Now hear once again the cry of the Spirit through this "watchman on the wall." To the dead or sleeping church, the Spirit cries, "Awake!" (Romans 13:11, Ephesians 5:14). To those who oppose this move of God, the Spirit warns, "Beware, lest ye be found opposing God!" (Acts 5:39). To those who have been awakened, the Spirit exhorts, *"Stay awake and alert with oil in your lamps and wicks trimmed* (Matthew 25:1-3)...*stand fast therefore in the liberty wherewith Christ hath made us free, and be not entangled again with a yoke of bondage"* (Galatians 5:1).

From years back, I have a tract that bore a strong witness with my spirit when the Lord got it into my hands. Based on Joel chapter two, it is entitled, "Where are the Weeping Intercessors?" During that special time (written about in Chapter five), my knees would hardly hit the floor of my prayer closet before I would begin to travail in intercession and when I came out of that holy place, a man's big handkerchief would be soaked. Now, that did not make me anything special. It simply meant God was getting His work done through me.

Dear reader, as you finish reading this book, I would encourage you to go back and re-read chapter one which so ties in with this final chapter. Those who have "eyes to see" and "ears to hear" will be able to sense that its message is more relevant now than ever before.

Revelation 5:10 reminds us that, as believers, we are all kings and priests (intercessors) unto God. Oh, may we be found faithful at our post of prayer! Again, we must repeat, eternal vigilance is the price we pay for freedom in Jesus Christ. Prayer constitutes vigilance and vigilance constitutes prayer. Heed the clarion call of Jesus, Himself, to watch and pray!

Maranatha! Even so, come Lord Jesus.

Amen.

Recommended reading:

The Jesus Style, by Gayle D. Erwin, Yashua Publishing

Impac Chris tian Books

332 Leffingwell Ave., Suite 101
Kirkwood, MO 63122